RELIGION'S PLACE *in* GENERAL EDUCATION

Religion's Place *in* General Education

by Nevin C. Harner

~~~~~~

INCLUDING

The Relation of Religion to Public Education:
The Basic Principles

•

A COMMITTEE REPORT
OF THE
AMERICAN COUNCIL ON EDUCATION

John Knox Press
RICHMOND, VIRGINIA

FOREWORD 〉〜

THIS timely analysis of one of America's most pressing problems was delivered in the form of four addresses during the Annual Midwinter Lectures at the Austin Presbyterian Theological Seminary.

Dr. Harner appeared on the Religious Education Foundation, sponsored by the Committee of Religious Education of the Synod of Texas, Presbyterian Church, U. S.

Insistent demand from lay people, ministers, and directors of religious education who heard Dr. Harner and appreciated his boldness in facing these issues with clean and deep insight, have called for this publication.

PREFACE ⟩∾

THE FOUR STUDIES of which this book consists have been allowed to retain substantially the lecture form in which they were presented to the faculties, students, alumni, and friends of two theological seminaries. Any disadvantage resulting therefrom will possibly be offset by a measure of directness which is necessarily involved in speaking to a visible and responsive audience.

I wish to record my sincere appreciation to President Frederick W. Schroeder of Eden Theological Seminary, St. Louis, Missouri, who first invited me to lecture in this area; and to President David L. Stitt of the Austin Presbyterian Theological Seminary, Austin, Texas, whose kind encouragement and assistance have been so largely responsible for bringing these lectures to publication.

Grateful acknowledgment is due also to the publishers who have granted permission for the use of the quotations indicated at various points throughout the following pages.

The interrelation of religion and education is such a live issue that it is in constant flux, and a statement set down today may be out of date tomorrow. An attempt has been made to take account of major developments up to the time of the final completion of the manuscript.

—N. C. H.

CONTENTS ⟩⟿

RELIGION'S PLACE *in*
GENERAL EDUCATION

CHAPTER I

RELIGION *and* EDUCATION
. . . INDIVISIBLE!

THE STARTING POINT for our thought may well be a memorable statement by L. P. Jacks: "If you want a man to think deeply and earnestly and with the fear of God upon him, set him thinking about education. He will soon find out, for example, that religion and education are not two things, but one thing; two only on the surface, but one in the ultimate foundations and the final aim."[1]

What can be the meaning of this puzzling statement? How can religion and education — commonly regarded as distinct and separate entities, each with its own principles, methods, and goals — be thought of as "not two things, but one"? Is it possible to enclose these two within a single framework of thought? Let us see. And let us proceed by inquiring whether it is possible to define these two, without doing injustice to the true nature of either, in identical words.

Religion has been defined again and again, and never to the full satisfaction of any large number of people. But perhaps as good a definition as any is to say that religion is a profound belief that the plan and purpose of God are made known to man, and an earnest effort to conform thereto. Where are the purpose and plan of God made known? The answer of classical Christianity is that this took place chiefly in a historical revelation, extending through the course of Jewish history and culminating in the person of Jesus Christ.

However, it is rarely denied that the natural and moral order also afford true glimpses of the divine nature and intention. And where within man's life and activity is the earnest effort made to conform to this plan and purpose? Primarily within the spiritual nature of each individual human being. That is the spot for a growing awareness of God's gracious purpose. There the response of faith is made. There the soul yields to the beckonings of divine grace, and gives itself fully to the processes of redemption and atonement. There the effort is made to live a moral life befitting the redeemed of God. And secondarily conformity is sought within the social arrangements of man's common life. Here, too, the will of God is to be discerned and performed. This, too, is fit material for redemption. This, too, must come under the sway of God's plan and become amenable to His purposes.

And now what about education? The strange fact is that education in its full stature can be defined in precisely the same words — namely, a profound belief that the plan and purpose of God are made known to man, and an earnest effort to conform thereto. Where are this purpose and plan made known? For those who have eyes to see, in the very structure of things, in the dynamics of human nature, in the so-called laws of learning, in the fundamental principles of human growth. These are laboriously discovered by man, and traced out in endless pedagogical textbooks. But man merely comes upon them; he in no sense creates them. They antedate any present generation of psychologists by hundreds of generations. They may be stated in words which contain no hint of their divine source, but that does not alter the fact that they originated in the mind and heart of God and truly express His plan and purpose for the lives of His children. The sensitive and devout educator, while beginning at this point in his discovery of God's intent, does not end here. It is needless folly for him to refuse to look also to historical revelation, which rightly understood cannot in any sense contradict God's self-disclosure in the structure of things, for God is one. And where within man's life and activity is the earnest effort made to conform to this plan and purpose? Not now within the confines of his own soul, but in his dealings with individuals less mature than himself; in other words, in the teaching process. That is the spot now for a growing awareness of God's gracious purpose. There the effort must be made to discern how God has intended life to grow, and to proceed accordingly. The place of discovery and the place of practice are measurably different; but the essentials remain untouched. Properly understood, religion and education are not two things, but one. Perhaps Jacks was right after all.

It goes without saying that religion can be stated, and often has been stated, in such a way as to make it non-educational, and utterly incapable of being included within the same thought-world as education. The way to accomplish this is tragically easy. The more God is lifted above His created universe, the more His transcendence is stressed to the neglect of His immanence, the more His operations are limited to miraculous and supernatural inroads into the world of the commonplace, the wider the gulf is made between God and man — the less possible it is to hold to the true kinship of religion and education.

Whenever and wherever this tendency goes too far, religion is the loser. The results can readily be traced in any era in which this tendency reigns supreme. Religion tends first of all to become otherworldly, supramundane, remote from the affairs of home, school, and market place. By the same token it runs the risk of losing its moral drive and relevancy. For man's everyday living ceases to be of primary concern. And besides, man himself is so belittled that not too much can be expected of him. The abject sinfulness of man is magnified to a degree that approaches the morbid. He is by nature "prone to all evil, and backward to all good," and "there is no health in him." Even his best actions and intentions are, unknown to him, corrupted and polluted by sin. Then it is that a priestly, professional class arise who are the custodians of the ineffable mysteries of God. With their sacrosanct robes gathered tightly about them, they move as citizens of another planet; and indeed they scarcely belong to this world. The Bible becomes a miraculous insert into the long processes of history, with no antecedents and no consequents. Its hidden truths are manifest not to the intellect but only to the eye of faith, which is unsealed by an operation from on high. Jesus Christ is a lone figure who is in history but not of it. The chief lines of communication between this everyday world and that other are the sacraments — two or seven as the case may be.

This is what happens to religion when it gives itself without reserve to the doctrine of God's transcendence. Such religion is a thousand miles removed from education. The two can scarcely be mentioned in the same breath. In order to keep religion on speaking terms with education, some true and authentic concept of God's immanence is required.

It goes without saying likewise that education can be

stated, and has often been stated, in such a way as to make it non-religious, and utterly incapable of being included within the same thought-world as religion. And, again, the way to accomplish this is tragically easy. The more God is immersed within His created universe, the more His immanence is stressed to the neglect of His transcendence, the more the vaunted powers and capacities of man are stressed, the more seldom humble reference is made to God as the high and eternal source of man's being, growth, and destiny — the less possible it is to hold to the true kinship of religion and education.

Whenever and wherever this tendency goes too far, education is the loser; and it matters not a whit whether it is so-called secular education or religious education which we have in mind. For now a different and opposite set of results comes into play, which can readily be traced in any period in which this tendency proceeds unchecked. The content of education is first of all sharply abridged and limited. It becomes exclusively this-worldly. It sees today and tomorrow, but not the far-reaching lifetime of an immortal soul. Likewise its goal is foreshortened and circumscribed. It is reduced to the level of the ethical alone, having much to say about the adjustment of man to man and of man to the world, but little or nothing about the adjustment of man to God. For there is no God left who is worth bothering about, or worth adjusting to. The innate goodness of man is exalted out of all reason, and with naïve disregard for the stubborn and abundant evidences of man's capacity to wreck his own life and his neighbor's. The educators themselves are cut adrift like ships on a mighty ocean with no home port from which they know themselves to have set out and to which in due time they will return, and with no unfailing heavenly light by which to plot their course. Moreover, they suffer from a pitifully impoverished view of what they are doing (and this, again, is equally true whether it be so-called secular education or religious education which we have in mind). The business of education in which they are engaged is a trifling matter of one human being doing something to another human being. There are no redeeming overtones of the divine, no sense of God's presence and purpose and power within the educational process, no saving recollection that the dynamic which changes life is after all God-given, and the rules by which life is changed are in the final analysis God-ordained. Only one human being doing something to another human being — simply that and nothing more! There is no lift to education so conceived, and no religion — even if it be called religious education. The Bible becomes an earthy book, the crystallization of individual and racial experience, the halting account of man's quest for a God who does not Himself join in the quest and whose very existence may be nebulous. Jesus Christ is a good man who said some startlingly beautiful things, and died a noble death, and climbed Godward — or perhaps just a good man. The sacraments are largely gone, and the sense of the sacramental itself is dissipated. There are no open highways between God and man.

This is what happens to education and life when the doctrine of God's immanence is pursued without reserve. Such education is as far removed from religion as the east is from the west. The two can scarcely be mentioned in the same breath. In order to keep education on speaking terms with religion some true and authentic concept of God's transcendence is required.

It is strange — is it not? — that the basic issue here as elsewhere is theological. When the concept of God moves too far in the *"ganz anders"* direction, God is abstracted from His created world and religion falls short of being educational. On the other hand, when God's immanence is carried too far, He is first lost in the meshes of His own creation, and then lost altogether, and the end result is an education which falls short of being religious.

One of the besetting sins of humanity, which in the long run is capable of doing perhaps as much mischief as the less subtle sinfulness catalogued in the Ten Commandments, is our inability to grasp at the same time opposite poles of thought and cling to them both at the same time in true dialectic fashion. To change the figure, a popular radio program some time ago had one of its characters remarking plaintively: "It's all right for the pendulum to swing, but there's no point in knocking the side out of the clock." There seems to be something in human nature which finds it easier to swing far out toward either extreme than to take a poised and balanced position midway. A good many of the schismatic divisions into which the church has fallen during its long history can be explained by this limitation of the human spirit. It would be interesting to explore this thesis further, if the time permitted (which it does not), and if the speaker were a student of historical theology (which he is not). More to the point of our present discussion is the fact that some regrettable mishaps in the area of the relation of religion and education within recent years seem to be understandable — partially, at least — on this basis.

For example, how did it come about that religion and public school education have so largely gone their separate ways in the United States? Such a separation has been virtually unknown among the nations of the world. Why then did it happen here? There are of course many answers, some of which we shall examine in more detail in our next chapter. There was doubtless to begin with the pattern of a secular state furnished by the French Revolution. And beyond this there was without a doubt the unprecedented diversity of our religious life, and a multiplicity of sects such as the world had never witnessed before, which made the task of incorporating religion within public education an almost hopeless one. But one wonders, as he looks back over the past century, whether there was not something more.

Could it be that, on a deeper level, during the very decades in which our public school system was taking shape two different cultures existed side by side? The one was the religion of the churches, whose God was enthroned on high and only intermittently walked the pathways of man's everyday life. And the other was a popular, this-worldly ideology, whose trend was in the opposite direction. Those were the years, we recall, of the flowering of science, when man was hypnotized by his own newly discovered powers and began to picture himself as "the master of his fate, the captain of his soul." After all, Charles Darwin, the most illustrious name in modern science, and Horace Mann, the father of the American public school system, were contemporaries. Their lives overlapped a full half century. Those, too, were the years of the marvelous spread of a new people throughout a new continent, free from Old World restraints, free to stand on their own feet, make their own laws as they went, and create their own futures. There was no bowing to the ground before nobility riding grandly down the road. There was no nobility, and not much in the way of roads. The Declaration of Independence is merely a precious document epitomizing a whole era. The mood of independence and of humanistic self-assurance was abroad throughout the land.

The educational implications of this mood were well described by Dr. George A. Buttrick in an address made recently before the Association of American Colleges: "Man is born free, but everywhere finds himself in chains. Therefore set him free; it is the prime task of education. Set him free politically, and he will vote himself into Heaven. (We cannot understand why he should choose Bilbo or Mayor Hague.) Set him free psychologically — his only trouble is a few inhibitions — and he will soon become a radiant personality. Set him free pedagogically, and even in the kindergarten he can write his own curriculum with the left hand while playing with blocks with the right hand. Set him free scientifically, and he will build a streamlined aluminum paradise. He is an angel in process of liberation. All he needs is facts and more facts. Information will of itself become knowledge, and knowledge somehow will become wisdom. Man is a long way from home, but his feet are on the road (called evolution), and if he is fed enough facts he will arrive in heaven. Progress is the word. It leads apparently to the grave, and perhaps to a cinder-planet; but let us ignore that fact. Progress, evolution, and freedom."[2] It was from such a soil that the public schools of America sprang during the nineteenth century.

And so the two cultures inhabited the same land and to a degree dwelt side by side in the same individuals, but they were poles apart. The one clung with an outstretched right hand to a sovereign, transcendent God; the other clung with its left hand to the doctrine of immanence with all its lovely and unlovely derivatives; and the two were drawn so far apart that they could not clasp their other hands together. It does no good now to look back and say that both were at fault. We are merely trying to understand, if we can, what has happened. How different the story might have been if neither side had gone so far, each driving the other to greater excesses in its own position and practice, and creating a deplorable rift in American life!

Or, to look at another mishap in the interrelation of religion and education, why is it that the church and religious education have so strangely drawn apart on occasion? There can be no doubt that they have drawn apart. In many a congregation the church and church school are separate institutions, each going its own way. The church school superintendent is almost a second pastor. I have seen instances where the two organizations were rivals for credit when something outstanding was accomplished. But the two are often separate not merely organizationally, but also ideologically. They use different hymnals, sing different hymns, pray different prayers, to a degree seek different goals by different methods. Some people attend only the one, and others only the other. There is a division of loyalties, and almost a twofold culture housed in the same building. Why is this? On the city, county, and state levels there have been until quite recently two parallel structures — an array of ministerial associations or church councils on the one hand, and a similar array of Sunday-school associations on the other. A stranger moving in succession from the one to the other would hear different vocabularies, and distinguish different outlooks. Why should this be? In theological seminaries, with some glorious exceptions, there is often a great gulf fixed between the department of religious education and the older disciplines, which no man can cross. The professors know it, the students know it, the alumni know it. I once heard a competent theologian say that he had had intimate contact with three theological seminaries in his lifetime, and this condition prevailed in all three of them. How do we account for such a condition?

Again, the explanations are many and various. It is worth while remembering that the first Sunday school was held in a house, not a church; and was started by a printer, not a minister. From the very beginning, therefore, a certain extra-church character has tended to inhere in the Sunday school. Also worth noting is the fact that the Sunday school has represented the greatest lay movement within Protestantism. Perhaps a part of the difference between church and church school is merely the difference between the lay and the clerical outlook upon life and religion and education. Furthermore, when the Directorship of Religious Education began to rise to the status of a separate profession, many of the new directors were trained not in theological seminaries but in graduate schools of universities, and the gulf was widened. But is this all there is to it?

Could it be that again we have to deal with two cultures,

existing side by side and separating on the same old basic issue? On the one hand was the church, the custodian of the historic supernatural faith. And on the other hand was the religious education movement, a child of this world, speaking the language of a scientific psychology, emphasizing work rather than worship, stressing the capacities for growth within the child rather than his sinfulness, and in short proving itself to be at every point on the side of God's immanence and all its corollaries. Again we may now look back and point out with all the proud assurance of a Monday morning quarterback that both were wrong, both went to extremes. But it does no good to assess blame. We are merely trying to understand what happened, and, where it was amiss, trying to see to it that it does not happen again. How different things might have been if a better balance had been preserved on either side!

The Study Committee of the International Council of Religious Education, whose work has just been completed, will doubtless prove significant in many respects. But perhaps one of its greatest services will be a contribution in the direction of fusing these two cultures into one, and bringing these two polar opposites — the transcendence of God and the immanence of God — into one balanced perspective. The very membership of the Committee was such as to make for this outcome. It included churchmen, theologians, religious educators, general educators. Bishops and psychologists sat together and whittled away at one another's excesses, to the probable advantage of both parties. This was the first time since the start of modern education that so many professionals on both sides of this ideological chasm were brought together

and held together for so long a time under the banner of religious education. One would expect a pretty fair synthesis
from such a procedure, and as a matter of fact we believe
it took place — to the lasting benefit of both religion and
education.

One of the most striking examples is the section on "The
dual nature of man." This, after all, is the acid test — namely,
the doctrine of man. Here transcendence will show its hand
inevitably, and immanence likewise with utter clarity. The
report of the Study Committee is manifestly neither the one
nor the other, but both. A quotation from Dr. Paul H. Vieth's
book, *The Church and Christian Education,* which is a popular presentation of the Study Committee's findings, will re-
veal this clearly: "Christian faith uses language peculiar to
religion in describing this twofold nature in man. On the
one hand he is a child of God, made in the divine image.
Within the bounds of human limitation, he is capable of
thinking God's thoughts after Him and of seeking to do God's
will. . . . But on the other hand man is also a 'fallen' creature.
The divine image has been marred. This is the truth which
is affirmed in the first chapters of Genesis. There are tenden-
cies to evil in human nature itself so that when man is left
to himself he does not find salvation. . . . The modern Christian education movement in its early days in this country had
a confident belief in the possibilities of Christian nurture for
the realization of Christian personality and the achievement
of a more Christian social order. In this confidence it was in
line with the beliefs of general education that in and through
adequate educational procedures the possibilities of man could
be developed. . . . The theological reaction which has pointed

again to the more tragic aspects of the human situation has been a disturbing challenge to the assumptions which underlay programs of Christian nurture. One of the greatest needs of religious educators today is to restore the proper balance between these two truths."[3] So reads the report of the Subcommittee on Theological and Educational Foundations, of which Professor John C. Bennett was chairman. When we find bishops and psychologists alike subscribing to such a statement, we can thank God and take courage. We are getting somewhere.

When these two equally valuable poles of thought — the transcendence of God and His immanence — are brought together in proper balance and tension, each supplementing and correcting the other, then education and religion move toward each other until they coincide indivisibly. When this happens, the way is cleared for religion once more to be incorporated within general education, of which we shall have more to say in our next chapter. When this happens, the ancient and ugly breach between church and church school is on the way to being healed.

In fact, when this happens, a whole series of beneficent results flow forth in a steadily increasing stream. In church and public school, in the pulpit and the youth fellowship alike, both this world and the world beyond become matters of tremendous concern. The life-situation which must be faced this afternoon becomes significant, and so does the destiny of a human soul ten thousand years from now. Time is important, but so is eternity — in church and school alike. The relations between man and man receive large attention in both, but so do the relations of man and God in

both. Work is assigned its proper place; and likewise worship, waiting upon the Lord. God has disclosed Himself
in a definite historical revelation, but He is still alive and at
work — "closer to us than breathing, nearer than hands and
feet." We turn the corner in the primary department, or in
grade 3-B, and He is there. Man is a child of God, but also a
sinner — and the two are said in the same breath. The historic sacraments are duly observed and reverenced as channels of divine grace, but every happening, every grouping,
every influence, is potentially sacramental and charged with
the divine. The Bible is a literary record of God's self-giving
approach to man, and of man's self-giving response to God.
Jesus Christ is true God and true man. God is not sufficient
without man, and man is certainly not sufficient without God.
"My Father worketh hitherto, and I work," is the way it must
always be put. The minister and the educator alike assert
their freedom, assume their responsibility without flinching,
but always as unto the Lord; and they rest back securely upon
the everlasting arms. Religion becomes educational, and education becomes religious. In short, religion and education
become what they always should have been and always should
be — namely, two sides of a single coin. What God hath
joined together, let not man put asunder.

In conclusion, it remains to suggest briefly the benefits
accruing to both camps from such a balance. On the one
hand, religion stands to profit greatly. Without losing its grip
for a moment on things heavenly, it is made to walk upon the
earth. The minister's sermons come to grips with the day-by-
day issues of life which his people face. He still continues to
proclaim the everlasting gospel, but he cultivates the art of

translating it into terms of twentieth-century city streets and country roads. His own training gets its substance in part from the tremendous past, but in part also from the tremendous present; and he thereby becomes a better servant of God and man. His pastoral work is illumined with the finest insights to be derived from psychology and sociology. The church's grand strategy becomes far more complete and adequate. It is no longer concentrated too heavily upon the preaching of the Word and the administration of the sacraments, as though these alone were the influences for the making of life. While keeping for them a place of highest honor, its vision is as wide as life is wide, and as broad as the mind of God itself. And so it concerns itself with home life, play life, work life, the interrelations of classes, races, and nations, because it knows full well that these are continually making and unmaking life. The patterns of worship are determined not merely by what was done in the first century or in the sixteenth, but also by the spiritual needs and hungers of men and women, boys and girls, in the twentieth century. The truths of modern psychology and education are too true and too well established to be passed by lightly. The church cannot afford to overlook any segment of God's truth, whatever its source. Religion is not fully religious until it becomes educational.

On the other hand, education also stands to profit immeasurably from such a balance. To put it colloquially, education receives a much-needed face lifting, a lifting of its face unto the hills from whence its help comes. Logically, in such a point of view there can be no such thing any longer as purely secular education. The very phrase is a contradiction in terms, a monstrosity which cannot longer be tolerated. All education, in this way of looking at the matter, must include religion within its purview, and thus achieve its full and rightful dimensions. We shall say more of this later. But religious education also is enlarged and corrected. It acquires a realistic view of the individuals entrusted to its care, challenging them to creative activity and calling forth all the good that is in them, but devising new methods for turning their faces toward the redemption they so sorely need from the sin which so constantly besets them. It gains a new respect for the Christian movement in history, including the Bible, the creeds, the ancient hymnody of the church, the art, the architecture, the martyrs and saints of all the ages, and uses these heavily in its teaching. It has little patience now with services of worship which are thinly emotionalized periods of self-examination and self-exhortation, but endeavors reverently to turn people's eyes toward the God of their salvation. In more ways than we can possibly list, education is not fully educational until it is fully religious.

It may be that this is something of what Jacks meant when he wrote: "If you want a man to think deeply and earnestly, and with the fear of God upon him, set him thinking about education. He will soon find out, for example, that religion and education are not two things, but one thing; two only on the surface, but one in the ultimate foundations and the final aim."

CHAPTER 11

THE PLACE OF RELIGION IN GENERAL EDUCATION

It IS NO SECRET that religion has been pretty well squeezed out of general education in the United States. Until the rise of Soviet Russia, we enjoyed the doubtful distinction of being the only country in modern times in which this development had taken place. Prewar Japan is sometimes added to the list, but Shinto has been such a complete interweaving of patriotism and religion and has held such a prominent place in the schools of that country that it is doubtful whether Japan should be included.

To be sure, a sincere and wistful nod is made quite generally in the direction of religious observance in our public schools in the form of the reading of the Bible, often a specified number of verses to be read without comment. A tabulation in 1941 revealed that in 12 states the law explicitly required such reading; in 6 others it permitted it; in 18 states the general terms of the law or else the law's silence made Bible reading permissible; in 8 states such reading was expressly forbidden; and in 4 more the ban was assumed.[1] But at best all of this represents only a gesture. By no stretch of the imagination would it be considered an adequate handling of reading, or arithmetic, or history.

Before going further we should hasten to say that this situation does not imply that our public school teachers and administrators, or our state university officials, are atheistic or irreligious. Quite the contrary is true. Many of them are devoutly pious individuals. The situation is not of their choosing or making. The fault lies elsewhere largely.

Why has this happened within a nation whose foundations are religious to so large a degree? We have already tried to suggest in the previous chapter what may have been a basic reason. Is it just coincidence that the American public school system developed through a succession of decades during which more and more in common thought God was being lowered from His throne in the heavens, the qualitative gap between Him and man was being narrowed, and confidence in the essential goodness of the student and the potency of the teacher was receiving increasing emphasis? The religion of the churches breathed an altogether different atmosphere, the high and lofty air of traditional Protestantism with its transcendent, sovereign deity. But Horace Mann, it may be noted, was himself a Unitarian. And beyond and beneath all churches and all divergent shades of religious doctrine, a secular culture was taking shape; and secularism is merely a conception of life without the upward look, without a God-reference. American public education, as we know it, may be regarded as an institutional expression of unbounded faith in man; certainly not an embodiment of humble trust in God. We have no desire to press this point too far, but it is worth some earnest meditation.

Having said all of this, we must go on to add that an intensely practical situation added fuel to the fire — namely, the excessive sectarianism of American Protestantism. To this new land came the founding fathers, bearing with them all the denominational types that had developed in the Old

Country, and adding some new ones of their own on this side of the Atlantic. It was this circumstance which finally led to the virtual elimination of religion from the public schools. It had not always been thus. One spelling book during the colonial period contained 148 pages of Biblical and religious material, as over against 20 pages of pure spelling.[2] Horace Mann in his first report after becoming secretary of the Massachusetts Board of Education in 1837 complained that he had found only three textbooks which conformed to the law passed a decade earlier forbidding sectarian texts, and these three were used in only 6 out of 2,918 schools.[3] The immediate occasion of the change, if not the ultimate cause, was the excessive divisions of American Protestantism, rendering any public teaching of religion — so it seemed — virtually impossible. Horace Mann himself was not irreligious, and was not averse to the teaching of religion in the schools. In a letter he said: "The religion of heaven should be taught to children while the creeds of men should be postponed until their minds are sufficiently matured to weigh evidence, and arguments."[4] He stood for Bible reading in the schools, for books embodying the principles of natural religion, and for the teaching of the precepts of morality and piety held by Christians in common. But the people of the churches were at one another's throats, and the educators gave up the struggle.

It was our own extreme individualism, our own insistence upon interpreting and worshiping God in our own private ways, that tipped the scales in favor of a dereligionized system of education. What an amazing circumstance that the Protestant Reformation, which in the first instance provided a mighty impulse for education of every sort, in its final bizarre consequences led to public schools with little or no religion! By the same token, a major remedy lies in the present ecumenical movement, whereby we hope to retrace some of the false bypaths into which Protestant individualism has led us and recapture a healthy measure of unity in belief, in worship, and in life.

We have paid a heavy price for our divisive freedom, which has led to the exclusion of religion from our schools. It may be that we do not fully realize how grievous the price has been. As ministers and churchmen we strive valiantly to reach the individuals of America with the Christian gospel. We establish a Department of Evangelism within the denomination, and experiment with new evangelistic techniques and approaches. But all the while the one agency which reaches all our children and youth for the greater part of their waking hours, nine months each year during the critical ages of six to sixteen, does little or nothing to make the coming generation religiously literate and responsive; and even conveys the negative suggestion in season and out of season that religion is really not important. Can we delude ourselves into thinking that any program for one hour or two hours a week, whatever its vitality, can stem this flood of constant influence? Can we dare to hope that we shall ever devise methods of touching the fifty percent of our population virtually untouched now by religion, so long as we fail to include in our planning the one institution which has them all in turn, and has them so long, and professes to include within its curriculum everything in life that is truly worth while? During the United Christian Education Advance a few years ago we were made to see the appalling picture of the schoolchildren of America — in rows of four, four feet apart — forming a procession across the continent from the Atlantic to the Pacific and all the way back again, and every other row without any systematic religious instruction whatsoever. Can we ever hope to reach those alternate rows for religion, so long as we fail to make some sound religious use of the public school? The labors of us all are made immeasurably harder and immeasurably less effectual than they would otherwise be. We work longer hours and achieve lesser results. We are practically foredoomed to disheartening failure and futility in our praiseworthy attempts to evangelize the unreached masses of America.

But this is not the end of the story. We are stymied also in our attempts to evangelize the social order, and bring it under the power of the Gospel. Here the curious and sorry illogic of our predicament reaches its climax. Dr. F. Ernest Johnson in an address once spoke to this point in substance as follows: Liberal Protestantism has characteristically tried to introduce ethical sanctions into the common life, but it has stood against religion in the public schools; hence it took away with one hand what it was trying to give with the other. Surely he was right. How shall we succeed in applying the sanctions of our religious faith to industry, to race, and to the world order, so long as we bypass the very place where matters such as these are treated at length — and with a taboo upon religion? Yes, we have paid a heavy price, heavier perhaps than we realize. The splendid idealism which goes under the heading of the social gospel, and the age-old passion for individual souls which we call evangelism, are alike frustrated in considerable measure so long as we fail to solve this problem.

Now what shall be done? If our thesis in the previous

study is at all correct, we must strive to find a way of putting religion back into general education not merely as an addition but as part and parcel of the whole process. It dare not be sectarian, but it can be definitely and warmly theistic. Without it, education is not fully itself; and neither is religion. How shall this be done?

The urgency of the problem has called forth a host of proposals. Many thoughtful people are disposed to feel that there is no way out except the establishment of parochial schools, wherein each denomination will once more integrate religion with education in its own way and with its own distinctive coloration. We intend to examine this proposal more in detail in the next chapter; therefore we shall not tarry with it now, except to say that it embodies difficulties and dangers which are truly formidable.

Some conclude rather fatalistically that the present situation has crystallized beyond all hope of change, and that therefore we can only redouble our efforts through the instrumentalities of the church and the home. But this is really no solution. It calls for merely more of the same. We have been working along these lines for a good many years, and the results leave a great deal to be desired. Surely we need to do more than we are now doing in church and home, and to do it better; but the question still remains, What about the public schools dotting every ward and every township throughout the land?

One of the most widely advocated remedies is the weekday religious education movement — classes in religion conducted by religious bodies on or adjacent to public school time. The following chapter will express the personal conviction that this is a sizable step in the right direction, but it is not enough. The addition of one hour a week of religious instruction is insufficient to compensate for twenty-nine hours of public school education whose texture is irreligious or non-religious.

A variant of this plan consists of classes in religion held within the public school building itself, and conducted by teachers employed by the religious interests of the community. The *International Journal of Religious Education* of June, 1944, contained a description of the outworking of such a plan in the state of North Carolina. At that time, 20,000 pupils were receiving such instruction in a hundred communities. The State Superintendent of Public Instruction was a member of the Committee on Weekday Religious Education within the State Council of Churches. The teachers were nominated by the churches within each community, and approved by the school board. The standards for their training and for their salaries were on a par with those of the public school teachers.[5] We may well rejoice in such a venture, but it is skating on very thin ice, and would scarcely work in any other than a homogeneous community. North Carolina is predominantly Protestant, with few Roman Catholics and few Jews. It is doubtful whether such a proposal would succeed in Boston or in New York City, and its legality is quite doubtful in view of the recent strong stand of the Supreme Court on the separation of church and state.

Another solution frequently put forward takes the familiar line of advocating that if the public schools cannot teach religion, they can at least engage in character education. Let them revamp their goals and their curriculum — so this proposal runs — in such a way as to make their supreme aim the cultivation of character. Let them work at this continuously through direct instruction as well as by indirection. Then they will at least be advancing the practical substance of religion, even if they cannot sound its metaphysical overtones. But this gives the case away. It is precisely the metaphysical overtones which we want. They are not some harmless extra, which can be retained or discarded at will, but the very heart of the matter. A flat, one-dimensional character education, which never dares to mention the will of God as the final source and resource of all attempts at ethical living, is like the play of *Hamlet* without Hamlet.

On occasion one hears the suggestion that the way out of our difficulty lies in the teaching of the religion of democracy within our public schools. Democracy, it is said, comprises a set of high and noble values which are accepted by virtually all our citizens and which involve no sectarian entanglements whatsover. Therefore, since religion in the traditional sense cannot be taught, teach the religion of democracy. Now no one can possibly object to education for and in democracy — the more of it the better; but this is not religious education. To say that it is constitutes an inexcusable confusion of language, of thought, and of policy. Democracy is not religion. It may be treated as though it were religion, and pursued with the deep devotion which is usually accorded to true religion (a like devotion is sometimes given to patriotism, or art, or the almighty dollar). But democracy is not religion, and education in democracy is not a substitute for religious education. If the substitution is attempted, the end result may be idolatry — the worship of the lesser instead of the greater, the

part in place of the whole. The solution does not lie in this
direction.

We return then to the search for a way of including true
religion within the curriculum of the public schools without
doing violence to the historic American principle of the separation of church and state. There would seem to be little
doubt that the solution is not to be found in terms primarily
of either doctrine or liturgy — both of these are prone to be too
sharply sectarian. We shall not be looking toward a course
in religion alongside of history, mathematics, and the rest. We
must endeavor to find something more fundamental and less
controversial than this.

The most likely proposal advanced thus far comes from
Dr. F. Ernest Johnson, who, as a member of the staff of the
Federal Council and also a professor at Teachers College of
Columbia University, is in constant touch with the thinking
of both churchmen and schoolmen. The suggestion is not his
alone; for, as we shall see, it is seconded by many eminent and
careful thinkers. But it has received perhaps its clearest and
fullest statement in his writings and addresses. It is utterly
free of all sectarianism. It does not violate the principle of the
separation of church and state. It gives no religious organization the slightest semblance of control over the schools (which
is the thing we must watch and fear). It seems to require
no new legislation, and no amendment of present legislation.
We can proceed to put it into effect, if enough of us have a
mind to do so. This proposal has been stated by Dr. Johnson
again and again, but we shall draw here upon the January 2,
1943, issue of *Information Service*, which was written by him
and devoted entirely to this matter.[6]

Dr. Johnson's thesis is that "religion can claim a place in the life and program of the school as an authentic phase of Western culture."[7] Religion can and should have a place in the curriculum of our schools, simply because those schools undertake to initiate each new generation into the living mysteries of the culture into which we are born and in the midst of which we live our lives, and religion is an inseparable part of our culture. In practical educational terms, this means that in every proper course religion will be included at its rightful place within the area of study under consideration.

Take history, for example. Dr. Johnson says: "How shall an American boy or girl come to understand the origins of American government without a knowledge of the faith that inspired it? . . . My plea is for as candid a study of the religious roots of our culture as we give to the secular — with no other purpose than to enable our youth to understand their own inheritance, and to appreciate it as such."[8] It is not merely irreligious, it is also unscientific, to try to present the story of American civilization with no fleeting reference to the religious motivations of our forefathers. Plymouth Rock with no allusion to religion is like a sentence without a verb, or geometry without the triangle, or a marriage without a bride. It is partial, incomplete, false, misleading, untrue. And so at every point the religious thread in history is to be traced as clearly and as fully as the economic, or the political, or any other. This, in fact, is the only way to teach history.

Or consider literature. Again Dr. Johnson writes: "In no aspect of the cultural heritage is the exclusion of religious studies from the schools more anomalous than in the failure to make our major religious classic, the English Bible, a part of

the cultural equipment of every generation. That the Bible
has been put to wholly unsound uses in religious education
may be freely admitted. . . . But is public education so desti-
tute of resourcefulness and courage that it cannot lay hold in
its own way on this matchless treasure of poetry and drama
and ethical prophecy in which the immemorial spiritual quest
of the race is recorded for our guidance, for our solace, and
for the strengthening of our hopes? . . . It should be taught
in the schools not as basis of dogma nor as substitute for science or history, but as literature, as *religious literature.*"[9]
Truly it is difficult to imagine anyone drafting a list of basic
English classics which does not include the King James trans-
lation of the Bible. Indeed it would be wholly unthinkable,
if we had not with our own eyes seen it done so often and so
long. And it is completely impossible to delete all religious
allusions and concepts from Browning, Wordsworth, Tenny-
son, and Shakespeare. Therefore, let us take our great literature as it is and teach it as it is — without evasion and without
apology.

Or turn to the social sciences. To quote Dr. Johnson once
more: "The schools should include in the social studies, precisely as they include other aspects of community organization, the institutions of organized religion. . . . No public
school pupil is being fully educated socially if while he studies
the government, the markets, the industries, the welfare
agencies of his community, he learns nothing of the characteristic ways in which that community expresses its spiritual aspirations in corporate ritual, meditation, and group
activity."[10] How strange it is, when we stop to think about it,
to take the young citizen and turn his attention carefully

toward every type of community institution — the bank, the store, the factory, the postoffice, the firehouse, the labor hall, the social settlement — with one glaring exception! In this conducted tour of the community in which he is to live and toward which he is to make the contribution of his own life, we develop a curious blind spot when we see a church or a synagogue on the corner. We must pretend that it really isn't there; or else that it doesn't truly count. And so we pass hurriedly by, and make our next stop at the city market. Of such a sort has been our teaching of civics. But now our teaching must be as wide as the community is wide, including the institutions of religion on exactly the same terms as all the rest.

We might go on to other fields — the natural sciences, for example. Every last one of them is saturated with religious connotations. All we have to do is free ourselves of our unnecessary inhibitions, and point them out. The fact that two atoms of hydrogen combine so invariably with one atom of oxygen to form water is not merely an illustration of chemical law — it is a miracle, an exhibition of divine grace and power. Who instructed the atoms how to behave? Who grouped the protons and electrons in such beautifully regular orbits? The chemist traces these phenomena, but he does not create them. Why not let him say so? Likewise the painful ascent of life through genera and species of ever-increasing complexity from the amoeba to man — "Some call it Evolution; others call it God." Why not take off our needless shackles and call it God, unashamedly and reverently, throughout the biological laboratories of our high schools and colleges? And so with physics, and with mathematics itself. It looks sometimes as though the Almighty must enjoy greatly playing with numbers. For instance, the sum of the first two odd numbers (one and three) is equal to the square of two; the sum of the first three odd numbers is equal to the square of three; the sum of the first four odd numbers is equal to the square of four; and so on forever and ever. Why not let the mathematician announce facts such as these with a sense of awe, as though he were touching the hem of the garment of the divine? — as indeed he is.

This is the gist of Dr. Johnson's thesis. Since religion is so inseparably a part of all life, let us stop trying to exclude it when we deal with any phase of life. Rather, let it enter when and where it will. We shall not need then an extra hour of religious instruction tacked on at the close of the day. It will have been there all the while — naturally, simply, inevitably, unmistakably.

Objections will of course raise their heads. One of the most obvious is that people will be afraid to have this done for fear that a sectarian twist may be given every treatment of religion. This is a risk we shall have to run. It may happen on occasion. But we need to remind ourselves quickly that we permit public school teachers to handle other phases of human concern in which there are wide and bitter differences among us, and we trust them to do it objectively. For example, here is a man who is registered as a Democrat. The chances are good that many of the teachers who instruct his two boys in history and civics from time to time are Republicans. But he raises no objection. He trusts them to deal fairly with the history and the present activity of all political parties. He does not suspect them of partisan propaganda at every turn. Their own individual leanings do not necessarily disqualify them as teachers, and he loses no sleep over the matter. The same is true of economics and a host of other areas. Why should it have to be different in religion?

Another objection is to the effect that all this is not enough. Of course it is not enough. As Dr. Johnson once said in an address, all that this can do is to predispose children favorably toward religion and lead them up to the church door of their choice. It cannot accompany them through the door into the Holy of Holies. There we must meet them as parents and churchmen, and take them by the hand, and bring them into the religious fellowship, and share with them the most precious things of our faith. But what an unmistakable blessing if such a program will only bring them to the door!

It is most encouraging to note the chorus of voices from many quarters endorsing the inclusion of religion within public education in terms such as we have outlined. The most notable statement on this subject ever issued is the recent report of the American Council on Education, entitled *The Relation of Religion to Public Education.* It was prepared by an inter-faith committee of fourteen members, of which Dr. Johnson was chairman. It is now released with the prestige of a great educational agency supporting it. No document in recent years is more deserving of careful study by ministers and Christian laymen. The full text of the report is included in this book, as an appendix, and critical comments by leading educators and churchmen may be found in the journal, *Religious Education,* the issue of May-June, 1947.

Dr. Luther A. Weigle, Dean of the Yale Divinity School,

has written: "There is nothing in the status of the public school as an institution of the state, therefore, to render it godless. There is nothing in the principle of religious freedom or the separation of church and state to hinder the school's acknowledgment of the power and goodness of God. . . . We must keep sectarianism out of our public schools. But that does not necessitate stripping the schools of religion. To exclude religion from the public schools would be to surrender these schools to the sectarianism of atheism or irreligion."[11]

Dr. Harrison S. Elliott, Professor of Religious Education in Union Theological Seminary in New York, has added his voice with words that re-echo almost exactly Dr. Johnson's position: "Leaders in the church school should join with public educators in developing a community sentiment which will enable public educators to introduce religion at the places it integrally belongs. For example, a class in social science studying the community must have the chance to study the church as well as the other institutions of society. A teacher of history must not be so filled with fear of arousing controversy that he cannot deal honestly and thoroughly with the manifestations of religion and of the church in history. A teacher of literature must not be kept from interpreting the religious experiences which are given expression in great poetry and great prose. Public educators must have the chance to deal with religion and the church as with other aspects of life."[12]

And re-enforcement comes from a high academic source in the person of Dr. Nicholas Murray Butler, the late president of Columbia University. Several years ago he wrote: "The separation of church and state is fundamental in our American political order, but so far as religious instruction is concerned, this principle has been so far departed from as to put the whole force and influence of the tax-supported school on the side of one element of the population, namely, that which is pagan and believes in no religion whatsoever."[13]

The recent full-length study of religious education conducted under the auspices of the International Council of Religious Education comes out at the same conclusion. On the last page of Dr. Vieth's book, *The Church and Christian Education*, in which he summarizes and interprets the work of the Study Committee, we read: "Many public school workers would be heartened if they knew that the religious leaders of the community could agree on co-operating with the public school in devising ways and means by which a school might give an interpretation of religion and religious institutions which would be given for all the children of the community."[14] We are merely trying to indicate that this position represents not the vagaries of one man's thinking, but a considerable consensus among statesmanlike leaders within both religion and education.

If this thesis is basically sound, what steps are needed to begin to put it into effect? We have already intimated our conviction that no legal changes are required. In a thoughtful article in *The Christian Century*, Dr. J. Paul Williams, who has made a painstaking study of this subject, says: "The public schools can do for religion what they do for politics: treat it descriptively. Religion could be taught descriptively, on school time, in non-sectarian classes, by teachers employed by the public — teachers who make a studied effort to do no more than *describe* religion. Such teaching is legal almost uniformly in the United States today; generally, the law prohibits not the teaching of religion but the teaching of sectarianism."[15] It would be premature to conclude that the Supreme Court decision in the Champaign Case has necessarily altered this situation, although further clarification might conceivably have this effect. Let us forget, therefore, the statute-books unless and until such clarification takes place; and let us turn elsewhere for the steps which are necessary in order to begin doing what we are permitted to do, what we want to do, and what we must do if the religious character of our civilization is to be preserved. Two steps are required in particular.

In the first place, much exploration of the matter is required in local, state, and national educational bodies. They do not all realize that this thing can be done, and done here and now. They do not all see the urgency of doing it, and doing it soon. Therefore, we must educate, and agitate, and cultivate without ceasing. We of the church must do this. We shall find many ready supporters within the ranks of schoolmen, but we must take the initiative. We must make friends of State Superintendents of Public Instruction. We must sit down and talk with them. We must invite them to speak at the conventions of our State Councils of Churches. And the same process must be repeated on the national level, and also on the community level. We ourselves can manage to be elected to our local school boards. It will be good for us, and good for the schools. And there we must press on toward our goal, not as members of a given denomination, or even as adherents to the Christian faith, but merely as good citizens convinced that this is the only way to preserve the indispensable religious foundations of our national life.

In the second place, a different type of teacher-training is called for. Our teachers' colleges, and the departments of education in our colleges and universities, are the seedbeds for the harvest which we hope to reap later. We shall need teachers favorably disposed toward religion, competently trained in religion, and thoroughly prepared to include religion within all their teaching in a manner calculated to be at once vital and inoffensive. Several years ago a young girl was attending a teachers' college in one of the Middle Atlantic States. On a week-end trip home she brought with her a history textbook, from which she was preparing to teach the children of the state. It purported to portray the whole course of American history, but the index contained only one or two feeble and futile references to religion. We must begin there, if we cherish any hope of arriving at the goal of an educational system which will make a rightful place for religion and all that it has meant and does mean to us, individually and socially.

This task to which we are called is not an easy one. It flies in the face of what is at present, and what many people firmly believe must ever be. But there is nothing in our commission as Christian disciples which exhorts us to ask whether or not a task is easy. Rather we must ask, Is it essential? Is it in accord with the will of God? Is it beneficial to the children of men? If the answer is "Yes," we go forward.

CHAPTER III

AN EVALUATION OF
CERTAIN CURRENT PROPOSALS

In THE PRECEDING discussion we endeavored to maintain the thesis that the only sufficient remedy for our deficiencies in religious education lies in the restoration of religion to an honored place within general education at every level — kindergarten, elementary, secondary, collegiate, and graduate school. Against the background of this conviction it remains to evaluate as honestly as we can certain proposals which are being advanced at the present time. As a matter of fact, they are more than proposals; they are practices, for they are already in operation in greater or less degree.

We are concerned here not with religious education in general — the church school, the confirmation class, the youth fellowship, and the like — but rather with that particular area within which religion and general education are tangent to each other. And we shall pass hurriedly over certain lesser suggestions which scarcely warrant full consideration.

For example, there is the plan of courses in religion offered within the public school curriculum for public school credit. This would seem to go both too far and not far enough. It goes too far in attempting to introduce religion into general education in terms of doctrine or Biblical content, which is probably the wrong way to go at the matter, and then giving official recognition for such study, which threatens to violate the principle of the separation of church and state. It does not go far enough in that it fails to interpenetrate all subject matter with religious meaning.

There is also the plan, tried in Pittsburgh and elsewhere, of offering school credit for attendance at religious service in the pupils' own churches. No matter how impartially it is administered, such a policy is in dubious accord with American tradition and established practice. Our major attention must be reserved for two proposals in particular — weekday religious education, and the parochial school.

The steel town of Gary, Indiana, is the birthplace of weekday religious education. A strange curriculum had arisen there about thirty-five years ago, which combined work, play, and study in one unitary pattern extending almost from sunrise till sunset. But this all-inclusive curriculum suffered from one omission — namely, religion. And so the far-seeing superintendent, a Mr. Wirt, entered into an agreement with the ministers of the community whereby some of the schooltime thus pre-empted would be released for the purposes of religious education.

The movement spread throughout the Midwest chiefly, until the depression of the 1930's. Then it languished for a while, only to enter upon a period of vigorous growth during more recent years. An improvement in economic conditions may be partially responsible for the new vitality within the movement, but that is scarcely the entire explanation. With democracy fighting for its very life, thoughtful observers began to fear for our democratic scheme of things no matter how the war turned out, if religion, the taproot of democracy, should lapse among our citizenry. And so there arose an almost desperate desire to strengthen the religious undergirding of democracy in any legitimate way, and the weekday school presented itself as such a way. There are now perhaps 2,200 communities offering weekday religious education to a total of approximately 2,000,000 boys and girls.[1] And our religious periodicals have been advertising steadily for more teachers for these schools. What now can be said concerning this movement, for and against?

On the credit side we must list first the fact that weekday church schools are succeeding in reaching a great many thousands of children who are otherwise untouched by formal religious influences. Dr. Vieth is authority for the statement that one-fourth of the pupils in these schools have not previously been in Sunday school.[2] One-fourth of 2,000,000 is 500,000 — a very substantial number. The percentage in many localities is even higher. In Lancaster, Pennsylvania, an old, established community of many churches, the proportion during the first year of weekday church schools was almost one half — 44% to be exact. In Virginia, where weekday religious education probably comes closer to universal coverage than in any other state, the percentage was exactly the same in 1942-43. One county of Virginia offered weekday instruction in religion to 1,038 children; of these all but 5 took advantage of the opportunity, and 62% of them had not been in Sunday school.[3] By and large it is not unusual for weekday schools to reach 90% of the available school population within the grades covered, whereas our church schools typically reach only 50%. There can be no doubt that this institution is genuinely effective in reaching the unreached.

To go a step further, the weekday schools have a good record at the point of turning children toward the church and the church school. At the end of the first year in Lancaster, the percentage of the weekday pupils without a church or Sunday school connection had been whittled down from 44% to 18%. That is a genuine gain. This record can be duplicated again and again. One teacher in Virginia reported an increase of 16% during the year in the number of her children attending Sunday school.[4] In other words, the weekday church school is an effective evangelistic agency, at least in the limited and easily measured sense of bringing people into a more vital relation with the church and its subsidiaries.

In the third place, the quality of the work done in the weekday school is commonly much higher than that of the average Sunday school, and tends to raise slowly the level of church school work. Not uniformly but frequently the weekday teachers are chosen in accordance with standards as high as those prevailing for public school teachers. They are paid for their services in many instances. In large school systems they have the benefit of helpful supervision. The paraphernalia of good education are often provided — blackboards, supplies, reference books, proper seating, lighting, and ventilation. Furthermore, the very proximity of weekday classes in religion to the public school makes for a certain carryover of mood and attitude, with an expectancy on the part of both teacher and pupils that serious work is going to be done. All of this is quite different from the typical Sunday school, as most of us have come to know it. But to a degree, the same pupils attend both. And to a degree, the same teachers serve in both. Thus the larger efficiency of the weekday school spills over, as it were, to the benefit of our older agencies of Christian nurture. In all probability from a pedagogical standpoint the best Protestant teaching in America is now being done in weekday religious classes. It would be strange indeed if these higher standards did not spread a little to other types of schools and classes.

A fourth advantage is to be found in the fact that weekday religious education promises to engender a measure of added respect for religion. This is accomplished in part by the process of organization and promotion which is required to establish and maintain weekday classes. The entire community is forced to give some new attention to religion. It is thrust upon their consciousness. It achieves a new stature in community life. Also, these schools by their very nature set religion alongside an institution which the pupil quite generally respects — namely, the public school. The same rules of attendance apply in both. As we have seen, the same standards of work tend to prevail in both. The school authorities co-operate in making a place for religious education. The net result is that religion tends to take on a new prestige in the minds of young and old alike.

A final entry on the credit side of the ledger lies in the precious extra hour of religious instruction which the weekday church school affords. The time at our disposal for the things of the spirit is so pitifully small that we cannot but welcome any addition from whatever source. One hour a week for half a million children is infinitely better than none at all. And two hours for the other million and a half is decidedly better than one.

This is an impressive array of advantages. Any institution with assets such as these to its credit deserves serious consideration and earnest support. However, in all fairness, we must turn over the page and have a look at the liabilities.

One objection frequently raised is that weekday religious education is merely an expedient, solving nothing. It does not take hold of the basic issue of making general education itself religious. Instead it merely adds one hour each week of religious instruction to twenty-nine hours, more or less, of unredeemed non-religious instruction. The more it succeeds, the longer we may evade the real issue, and therefore the more critical our plight. There is much truth to this contention, as has already been intimated. It may, indeed, be only an interim plan, which will be rendered superfluous once our whole educational system recaptures some real religious content and motivation. Meanwhile, and the interim may be longer than we desire, a patchwork, partial plan is better than nothing. In education as in life we often have to move forward for a time with expedients, temporizing measures, the best available at the moment. The work of the Lord has been done from time immemorial with imperfect tools. The part of wisdom is to be grateful for them and employ them to the fullest, until the more perfect makes its appearance.

Educational theorists often find fault with weekday religious education on the ground that it adds one more separate and uncorrelated educational experience to the many already in existence for the average child. Home, church, school, Boy Scouts, Y.M.C.A. and Y.W.C.A. — their name is legion. Each has its own program. Each pulls and tugs at the child in its own interests. And now we add another, unrelated to any previously in the field, and thus make confusion worse confounded. If a confession is in order, this observer finds it hard to get as excited over this pedagogical refinement as perhaps he ought to. Suppose the weekday classes pursue a program whose subject matter is utterly remote from anything that goes on elsewhere in the child's life (a supposition which is contrary to fact on the face of it), is that too horrible a fate for children? If the program is intrinsically good and worth while, it will do them good. And they will find some links between this and all the others in the unity of their own experience and in the fundamental continuity of community life.

Correlation is scarcely the greatest word in either education or religion. And lack of correlation is not the sin against the Holy Ghost. Furthermore, there need be no lack of correlation. In denominational weekday classes there can be genuine integration with the Sunday church school curriculum. Many a quarterly has expressly provided for it. The weekday hour can be a continuation of the session of last Sunday, and a preparation for the coming Sunday. And in both denominational and interdenominational classes there is abundant opportunity for correlation with the public school curriculum. In Oak Park, Illinois, and in other centers fruitful experiments have been conducted in developing a weekday religious education curriculum which marches hand in hand with the public school curriculum week by week. Two examples may be given, both of them taken from Oak Park. One teacher in an 8-A class "used the same classics that were studied in the public school literature course, and helped the students to evaluate their ethical and moral characteristics." Another eighth-grade teacher reports: "As the class studied American history in their social studies, we studied American *church* history to discover the contribution which the churches and their leaders gave and are now giving to American democracy."[5] Dr. C. A. Hauser, for many years on the staff of one of our denominational Boards of Christian Education, made a detailed analysis of the curriculum in use within the public schools of Philadelphia to discover latent religious values in the several courses, grade by grade, prescribed within that school system.[6] Such a study offers innumerable springboards for weekday religious instruction related intimately to the content of general education. In Virginia the public school theme for the third grade is "The Adaptation of Life to the Environmental Forces of Nature"; the weekday religious course for this grade is entitled "At Home in God's World." In the sixth grade the weekday religious course is "Spiritual Guidance in a Machine Age" to match the public school theme, "The Effect of Mass Production Upon Our Living." In so far as correlation is essential, we can achieve a large measure of it — if we set our minds to it.

Another objection sometimes voiced embodies the fear that the weekday schools will heighten the self-consciousness of religious and cultural groups by sending the Jewish children in one direction for their hour of religious instruction, the Roman Catholics in another, and the Protestants in yet another — or several others. Up to this moment they have been inseparable and indistinguishable in the great melting-pot of American democracy — the public school. But now they are sorted out, segregated, and made unhappily aware of their differences. This contention also is not without some justification. Because it is realistic and deals with things as they are, the weekday school may inevitably drive some narrow wedges between groups. A study made for a doctoral thesis at Yale

University indicates that this has actually happened in some communities where there was no adequate public interpretation of the released-time plan.[7] But, by way of compensation, it may accomplish the opposite effect through the circumstance that many of the weekday texts devote large attention to a sympathetic interpretation of other denominations, races, religions, and cultures. Besides, long before the Jews, Roman Catholics, and Protestants go their several ways to their respective classes, the rabbis, priests, and ministers have had to unite in the common cause of providing religious nurture for all the children of the community. So that what is taken away with one hand may be given back in generous measure, pressed down and running over, with the other. The study referred to above found, on the whole, some increase in mutual understanding and appreciation in the communities that had weekday schools. If weekday religious education were the only divisive force operating in America, we should have little to fear.

The final entry on the debit side of the ledger is by all odds the most considerable and the most conspicuous — especially since the Supreme Court decision in the Champaign Case. It is the serious misgiving that weekday religious education may constitute a dangerous invasion of the separation of church and state. In fact, some reputable observers apparently have concluded that all released-time classes of religion are banned by the recent Supreme Court decision. But the International Council of Religious Education, which has played an active role in the promotion of weekday religious education, does not at this writing accept this interpretation.[8] The confusion probably arises from the fact that several separate opinions were handed down by the Court. In addition to the official decision, four Justices signed a supplementary opinion in which they expressly stated that they were not passing upon the legality of the released-time principle per se. When account is taken of the further fact that one Justice was in dissent from the Court's majority opinion, it seems clear that five of the nine Justices are not now willing to declare released time illegal in itself.

Obviously this decision will have a far-reaching effect upon the weekday religious education movement. Classes may no longer be held in public school buildings (unless perchance the payment of an adequate rental fee would obviate this difficulty). And the public school's administrative machinery may not be used for recruiting, enrolling, staffing, disciplining, or grading weekday classes in religion. But three-fifths of these classes have already been meeting elsewhere than on public school property, and the others in their quest for alternative meeting places may actually strengthen the movement rather than weaken it. The remaining adjustments are by no means difficult to make. Pending further possible adverse rulings or interpretations, the great bulk of the weekday religious education systems throughout the country seem likely to continue.

Properly administered, weekday religious education contains no threat of sectarian control over the public school. It uses not one cent of tax money for sectarian purposes. It involves no official discrimination for or against any religious group. If it erred at any of these points, we would have cause to fear; but it does not — when properly administered. A person, therefore, who believes in religious freedom with all his might can support weekday religious education with a clear conscience. If this were the chief hazard in our nation to our precious liberties, we could be happy indeed.

It will be apparent, presumably, where the author's sympathies lie in this whole matter. The weekday church school is not, we hope, the last chapter of the story. But it is a heartening and rewarding episode in the middle of the book.

We turn our attention now to another proposal and practice in the area of the interrelation of religion and general education — namely, the parochial school. The Roman Catholic Church, of course, has long been the chief sponsor of such schools, and has regarded them as indispensable to its purpose and strategy. But there have also been Protestant parochial schools from the beginnings of American history. When the first struggling settlements took root along the Atlantic seaboard, it was typically in the Middle Atlantic States, rather than in the South or in New England, that parochial schools flourished. The memory of many schools of this sort is still cherished in Lutheran and Reformed circles in Pennsylvania. The founder of the Reformed Church in the United States, now a constituent part of the Evangelical and Reformed Church, was John Philip Boehm — a schoolteacher first and an ordained minister later.

But then the rapid growth of the American public school system under Horace Mann and his colleagues and successors almost entirely displaced the parochial school among Protestants, except for a limited survival among certain denominations. It may be interesting to note that in 1847 the General Assembly of the Presbyterian Church voted to promote parochial schools. Two hundred and fifty schools were actually started in twenty-nine states and the District of Columbia; but the attempt was not successful. The latest religious census, that of 1936, reveals thirty-one Protestant bodies maintaining parochial schools at that time, with a total enrollment of 275, 643. Of these, 180,865 were Lutherans.[9] The percentage of Roman Catholic youth attending their own parochial schools is given by Moehlman in his book, *School and Church,* as forty-three per cent. This represents a falling off from the peak year of 1926, when forty-eight per cent of Catholic children five to seventeen years of age were in parochial schools.[10] Now one hears considerable speculation to the effect that this type of instruction must be revived on a wide scale, as the only adequate way of coping with our present situation.

There can be no doubt that the parochial school presents the distinct advantage of overcoming completely the unhappy divorce between sacred and secular in education, and opening the way fully for an education shot through and through with religion from center to circumference. In a school conducted by a given denomination not only can there be full treatment of religious content in every proper subject, but there can also be out-and-out courses in doctrine with all the denominational coloring that is desired, as well as services of worship, and religious tests for the teaching and administrative staff. In short, the parochial school offers a complete and unhampered solution of our perplexing problem. One of the most persuasive arguments for this solution takes its start from the fear that we may be well on our way to losing our distinctive Protestant heritage. Therefore, we must take drastic steps to meet a serious situation. We cannot afford to dally with measures that are too little and too late.

It is the price involved which gives us pause. Are we willing to pay this price? Suppose that all the children of America were to be educated in Roman Catholic schools, Jewish schools, Evangelical and Reformed schools, Episcopalian, Presbyterian, Lutheran, and Methodist schools — what then? Such a situation would constitute a fatal threat to our national unity, far greater than that involved in a mere one hour a week of weekday religious education. It would accentuate and aggravate the divisions among us instead of healing them. Protestant would be arrayed against Catholic, and Gentile against Jew. Furthermore, it would drive ugly wedges between the various branches of Protestantism and defer to the distant future our hope of realizing the ecumenical dream. Do we wish to pay this price?

Suppose that we throw our energies into the establishment of parochial schools. The way is already cleared for a measure of tax-support to Catholic schools. We would, of course, claim the same privileges for our own Protestant schools of many denominational affiliations. That would expedite the next Catholic move—full tax-support for parochial schools. We, of course, would take advantage of this also. And that would probably be the end of the public school system in America, sooner or later. The prospect before us is scarcely one of a fairly intact public school system with a limited number of parochial schools in addition; rather it is the virtual displacement of the public schools by a set of sectarian schools. And that, as we have said, spells the doom of the American dream and of the ecumenical dream as well. When we set foot upon this path, we do well to look ahead to its farther end. This forecast, of course, is open to question. The future might not work out in this fashion. But the risk is there, and it must be appraised while there is yet time.

There is also inherent in the parochial school a far-reaching threat to our religious liberty, which arises indirectly from the present moves of the Roman Catholic Church toward securing tax-support for their parochial schools. In 1929 a Supreme Court decision opened the way for the use of public funds to provide textbooks in parochial schools. Six states have taken advantage of this decision and acted accordingly — Kansas, Mississippi, Louisiana, New Mexico, Oregon, and West Virginia. In 1947 a five-to-four decision of the Supreme Court legalized the use of tax funds for bus transportation to parochial schools on the doubtful ground that such an expenditure falls under the head of public welfare rather than education. *The Christian Century* views with alarm the whole proceeding, and not without cause.[11] For this is merely the entrance of the camel's head within the tent to be followed in due time by the entire body. The ultimate objective of Roman Catholicism seems clearly to be the securing of full tax-support for its educational system. If it is successful in this effort, its relative position in American life will be greatly strengthened. It already exercises a political influence out of proportion to its numbers. We do well to remind ourselves, without bigotry or bitterness, that the settled policy of Roman Catholicism favors complete religious liberty only where it represents a minority. Wherever it can do so, it feels obligated to suppress all other teaching than its own, in the interests of what it regards as revealed and final truth. All of this is worthy of consideration in deciding whether or not we wish to propagate parochial schools.

There are also certain practical difficulties to be faced in the parochial-school idea. In communities of small and moderate size, what would the weaker denominations do? The Methodists could conceivably establish their own parochial institutions almost at will; and the Evangelical and Reformed could do the same in St. Louis, in Cleveland, and in Philadelphia; and the Presbyterians in Pittsburgh, Chicago, and elsewhere. But there are many localities where any given denomination is not strong enough to maintain a school; what then? And what would be the policy of the smaller sects? Would they be forced into some sort of combination, and thus find their own way toward Christian unity — precisely contrary to what we have just said above? Or would they send their children to schools of the more fortunate denominations, and thus gradually pass off the American scene?

Even in large cities, there are difficulties in prospect. A child might have to travel far across town to reach the school of his own communion. And there would almost inevitably result a multiplication of schools, which would be less economical than our present system, and lead in turn to a lowering of the level of education. Many states and communities are experiencing real difficulty even now in paying teachers a satisfactory salary, until nothing short of an educational crisis is upon us. What would be the result if we divided our forces and multiplied our expenditures? And in the average church who will supervise so pretentious an educational undertaking? And, unless and until tax funds are used for this purpose, how can children of limited means avail themselves of the advantages offered?

We should think a long time before committing ourselves to this remedy. Our condition calls frantically for remedying, but the parochial school may be somewhat like the sulfa drugs — effective but dangerous. A few church leaders are exploring the advisability of church day schools limited strictly to younger children — nursery, kindergarten, and perhaps the first several grades. So long as the venture remains on the pre-school level the dangers and difficulties may be slight and the advantage genuine. But when it invades the public school years, both dangers and difficulties seem to apply; and the further it goes, the more they apply.

Some of us have had to wrestle with the question, How on these premises is one to justify denominational colleges? Do not the same lines of reasoning apply in the one case as in the other? To a degree, yes; but there are some marked differences.

Sectarian institutions on the collegiate level do not offer the same divisive threat as on the elementary and secondary level. Students who have been in the melting-pot for twelve school years, where there was neither Jew nor Gentile, barbarian nor Scythian, bond nor free, are not likely to become narrowly partisan and sectarian at the age of eighteen. Their formative years have been spent otherwise; they are steeped in community and universality; they may now with less danger come apart for a few years into an atmosphere shaped by their own communion. It is still necessary, of course, for church colleges to avoid all prejudice and bigotry as they would avoid the plague; but they could not, if they would, undo the impress of all the preceding years.

Further, while we greatly need religion-filled education at the elementary and secondary level, in certain respects we need it even more at the collegiate level. It is true that these earlier reaches of life are the time when character and personality are in the making, and we desire ardently to have religion introduced into that process. We have said this not once but many times. However, the public school is not the only influence in the lives of children from six to eighteen years of age. During these years they are still at home. If the homes are religious, they counterbalance in some measure the negative and opposite effects of secular schools. And during these years children are still potentially within reach of their home churches. If these churches reach them, and hold them, and shape them, something can be done to counterbalance the absence of religion in the schools. But when students go away to college, a change occurs. They are now no longer in constant touch with either their homes or their home churches. The college is the all-encompassing environment of their lives, in which they live, and move, and have their being. If it is saturated with religious influences, well and good. If not, the loss is considerable. They may or may not find for themselves a church home in the new environment. They may or may not stumble into a circle of student associates with an active interest in religion. They may or may not take courses in religion. Quite often they will not, unless these courses are duly emphasized and required on the same basis as courses in English or History or any other essential field. A revealing study has recently been completed by Dr. Edward W. Blakeman, Counselor in Religion at the University of Michigan. He tabulated the registrations for courses in religion within 102 colleges in the three states of Pennsylvania, Illinois, and California. In the church-related colleges they numbered 985 for every thousand students. In private colleges they fell to 562, and in public colleges to the very low figure of 84.[12] It means a good deal, therefore, to these adolescents to be placed at a formative stage in their lives within an environment which is avowedly and consciously religious.

Finally, the several denominations have a particular interest in higher education for the training of professional full-time Christian workers — ministers, missionaries, directors of religious education, and the like. It still appears to be true that most of our ministers received their academic training in church colleges — generally of their own denomination, sometimes of another. The truth of this statement can easily be put to the test by checking the ministers known personally to us in the *Yearbook* of our church, or by examining the catalogues of our theological seminaries to see where the students received their pre-seminary training. Any communion has a special stake in higher education, for the maintenance of its own professional leadership. For this reason among others, on the foreign mission field we commonly conduct lower schools in backward fields such as Africa or China where no other education worthy of the name exists. But in areas more advanced culturally, such as Japan, our major educational effort is pitched on a higher level.

And so there would seem to be no serious inconsistency in maintaining in the same breath the importance of denominational colleges and seminaries, and the questionable wisdom of establishing elementary and secondary parochial schools.

The conclusion to which these considerations leads us is that the parochial school does not represent the best way out of our difficulty. In countries which are fairly homogeneous religiously, or which are so far advanced in religious unity as to have a state church — England, for example — it may work satisfactorily. But our diversity is so great that we need to retain one place where it is forgotten and overcome in unity. A temporary way out, altogether useful for a time, is weekday religious education. But the only satisfying, lasting solution lies elsewhere. It consists in the reintroduction of religion as an integral part of all education on the one hand; and on the other in a revitalization of the church's own program of religious education. To this latter subject we shall turn our attention in the final chapter.

CHAPTER IV

THE DISTINCTIVE EDUCATIONAL TASK OF THE CHURCH

No EXTRA-CHURCH PROVISION for religious education, however adequate or well-conceived it may be, can absolve the church of its basic educational function and responsibility. If the thesis with which we began these studies is correct, religion at its best is so close to education that it is inescapably educative. Certainly the Christian movement in history has been haunted in every era with a never-failing sense of its teaching mission. The list of the measures it has developed over the years to discharge this obligation is long and impressive. Catechetical classes to begin with, and then monastic schools, cathedral schools, a renewal of catechization during the Reformation, the Sunday school, Christian Endeavor, youth societies and fellowships galore, men's groups, women's groups, forums, visual aids, academies, colleges, and seminaries, the publication of quarterlies, leaflets, magazines, and books — all of these testify to the utter inability of the Christian church to escape its role as educator. The record is a glorious one, which must never be allowed to stop. No matter what is done elsewhere, there are certain educational tasks which the church alone must perform, arising from its past history, its present situation, and its impulse to continue and to spread to the ends of the earth. Our purpose here is to look at several of these inalienable tasks, one by one.

In the first place, within any conceivable future the induction of each succeeding generation into the distinctive Christian heritage must remain the peculiar task of the church. This heritage is one of the abiding glories of our sadly shaken planet. Without a knowledge of it, any growing individual is the poorer. And without its intelligent perpetuation, the church itself cannot live. And because it is the property of the Christian community rather than of all mankind, and because it is handed down somewhat differently from denomination to denomination — like the same ray of light coming through different panes of colored glass — the church itself must see to the matter.

This includes the Bible. We have talked a great deal about teaching the Bible, and prepared thousands of quarterlies which purported to do nothing else but teach the Bible, and taken potshots at anyone who seemed to be neglecting the Bible in education, but we still have not taught the Bible. In a high school Biblical test administered to 18,434 students, 16,000 of them could not name so many as three of the Old Testament prophets; 12,000 could not name the four Gospels; and 10,000 could not name any three of the disciples of Jesus.[1] We might as well face the bitter fact: the Bible, which is the chief literary item in our Christian heritage, is "The Book Nobody Knows." And so, as a church, we must introduce our people to the Book, using the best scholarship of which we are capable, carrying our pupils with the aid of a sanctified imagination back into times long since gone and characters long since dead until both times and characters throb with life, and finding therein the living word of God to man.

This includes also the explicit teaching of Christian doctrine, not as the compulsory indoctrination of helpless minds with verbal formulae, but as the mature explication to and with each new generation of the great fundamentals by which the church lives. Doctrine is the intellectual expression of the church's very soul. It differs measurably from group to group. It is not the same among Protestants as it is among Roman Catholics. Presbyterians stress some things which Disciples and Episcopalians do not, and pass lightly over others which they cherish deeply. And so we must envision a vital and untrammeled exposition of the everlasting realities of the Christian faith — God, Jesus Christ, sin and salvation — as they are understood by a particular Christian community.

This includes likewise teaching about and experience with the liturgy. Worship is perhaps the most characteristic act of the Christian fellowship. If doctrine is the Christian community thinking, worship is the Christian community on its knees. The very word "liturgy" means the work of the people. It, too, differs markedly from Protestant to Catholic, and from one Protestant denomination to another — in fact, even from congregation to congregation. And so each particular fellowship of believers must interpret to its oncoming members the sequence, the rationale, the unfolding logic, the historic richness, of its accustomed ways of worshiping the Lord in the beauty of holiness. And it must go beyond mere discussion and explanation; it must discover ways of leading childhood and youth step by step into full and active participation in the liturgy. This necessary educational task is one of the most difficult confronting the church, for our forms of worship are the devotional expression of adult religious experience. Our hymns are the outpouring of adult faith; our prayers are the petitions of adult need; our confessions call the roll of adult sins in age-old phraseology far more intelligible to adults than to children. But we must persevere in the task nevertheless, else the sacred fires on our altars will dim and grow cold.

This includes, further, painstaking instruction in every phase of the rich heritage and tradition of the church not hitherto mentioned. The stream of Christian history itself deserves attention — the early centuries red with the blood of martyrs, the medieval period with its strange pattern of lights and shadows, the new birth of the Reformation, and the course of events on our own continent. And there is biography, the apostles and saints of all the ages — Paul, Augustine, St. Francis, Luther, Zwingli, and Calvin, Carey and David Livingstone. And there are art and architecture, music and symbolism. These all are our inheritance. We have received them from our forefathers, and we have the unspeakable privilege and obligation of transmitting them lovingly to our children.

This induction into our Christian heritage includes finally an adequate acquaintance with the present-day organization and far-flung program of the church. What is the church like as a present reality? Who are its officers? What are its subdivisions? What institutions are owned in its name? What is its work in America, in Asia, in Africa? How does it undertake to perform this work? And how are the denominations conjointly making headway toward the ecumenical dream of the day when there shall be one fold and one Shepherd?

All of this constitutes the first portion of the church's charter for Christian education. It comes down out of the past into the living present, and flows through us into the future which is yet to be. Lest there be some misunderstanding, we may hasten to make clear that this emphasis upon our heritage does not abrogate the person-centered principle, which has rightly become precious to many of us. Why do we cherish these elements of our heritage, and endeavor to weave them into the experience of the present generation? Not because we think they have any worth in and of themselves, but because we believe sincerely that they are indispensable to the fullest spiritual development of our children and our children's children. For a person achieves his fullest growth not in a vacuum, but in the context of the past, the present, and the future. As the report of the International Council's Study Committee puts it: "This viewpoint . . . sees at the center of the curriculum an individual learner, not in splendid isolation, but in vital relation to the great realities of the Christian faith and life — God, Jesus, fellow men, the Bible, the church, the world."[2] So we are not forgetting persons; we are merely bringing out treasures, old and new, for the enrichment and development of their lives.

In the second place, the church has the distinctive task of drawing out the ethical meanings of the Christian faith in terms of the various issues of personal and social living. There is a moral "plus" — difficult to define yet altogether real — which the Christian gospel and the Christian outlook upon life has to contribute to virtually every ethical issue. It is somewhat akin to the additional touch of genius which separates a Fritz Kreisler from a run-of-the-mine first violinist in a symphony orchestra, or a Paul Scherer from an ordinarily able and devout metropolitan preacher. This higher level of interpretation and meaning is not forthcoming in a mere sociology class, or economics class, or civics class — even when they are taught from a theistic point of view.

Consider, for example, the relationship between the sexes. Here the law has its own invaluable contribution to make, and likewise medicine, psychology, and sociology. But when all of these have had their say, there is still a place for the Christian insight that marriage is a sacrament or a near-sacrament, in which two individuals are joined in body and in soul for their own good and their children's good and the working out of God's purposes for mankind. In the words of the familiar advertising slogan, "something new has been added," which lifts the whole consideration of premarital and post-marital relations to a higher level.

Or, take the matter of vocational choice and vocational guidance. A host of new and promising techniques have been developed for helping the individual to analyze himself and the job, and to match the two in the light of the best scientific knowledge. But it remains for the Christian teacher to uncover the etymology of the word "vocation" — a calling, a calling from God to utilize one's talents in the service of His kingdom. And, lo, the whole procedure is luminous with new light, and transfigured with new meaning.

The same is true concerning the getting, the saving, the spending, and the giving of money. The economist has full right to be heard on this point, as does the social scientist, and even the originator of hard-headed and canny aphorisms, like Benjamin Franklin. But the Christian goes on from there to enunciate the principles of stewardship, and how the picture is altered! Now the possessions which we say we own are not our own; the talents by which we acquire them are merely placed in our keeping as a sacred trust; and all we have and all we are must be so utilized as to set forward the purposes of Him who is the Giver of every good and perfect gift.

When we move into the realm of social issues, the situation is in no wise different. The anthropologists, for instance, have much to tell us concerning race which we do well to heed. We are most grateful for such a monumental work as that of Myrdal on the Negro in American life. But only in Christian teaching do we rise to the lofty conception that racial differences are not a barrier to interrupt human fellowship, but a God-given variety to enrich it for which we should be profoundly thankful. And only in Christian documents do we encounter such strange counsel as: "Bear ye one another's burdens, and so fulfil the law of Christ."

The law of Christ is indeed above and beyond all other laws and formulations known to us. It extends even to the realm of international relations, which have plagued us so unceasingly in these recent years and now threaten to undo us all. No non-Christian source can give us such a report on war as that which proceeded from the Commission of the Federal Council. It spoke a language which, sad to say, fell strangely upon the ears of many people, because they had not heard it often enough and long enough. It is the distinctive function of the church in religious education to speak this language without apology or compromise on every ethical issue of individual and social life.

In the third place, the church has the peculiar educational

task of confronting each individual with the full-scale Christian gospel and the unmistakable call to Christian discipleship. This has been called, from time immemorial, evangelism. Here on the one hand is the gospel — the good news of God's love for mankind, the assertion that He has given and is giving Himself without stint for their redemption — and the call to men, "The time is fulfilled, and the kingdom of God is at hand: repent ye, and believe the gospel." On the other hand are persons — men and women, boys and girls, sinful and needy — waiting for a deliverance which they cannot achieve but can only accept, hungry for Someone and something to which they can give themselves without reservation. To bring these two hard up against each other is, and always will be, evangelism. Only now we are thinking of accomplishing this through educational means, educational evangelism. It is to be done through the instrumentality of preachers and teachers, parents and group leaders, who are themselves gospel-filled and gospel-inspired, living epistles "known and read of all men." It is to be done through teaching for a decision, which goes far beyond the mere impartation of facts to the deeper meanings of those facts for each individual life, and issues in a clear call to take a stand and make a decision. It is to be done in the course of a three months' study of the life of Christ, or the history of the church, or the meaning of church membership. It is to be done through worship services which bring individuals face to face with the Lord of their salvation. It is to be done in a confirmation class, which leads each confirmand to give a reason for the faith that is in him, and to decide for or against being on the Lord's side. It is to be done through preaching, drama, visual aids, exploration of the meanings of the gospel for everyday living, projects of service to persons and causes in need of human aid, wholesome recreation, and all the means by which each new individual is made a full member of the Christian community, so that its life courses through him and he enters more and more fully into its life. This is evangelism through education, educational evangelism.

In the final analysis, only the church can perform this function. As we have said earlier, a public school system which is once more permeated with religion can bring a boy or girl up to the very door of the Christian fellowship, but it cannot accompany him inside. There the church must take over. It must grasp him by the hand and invite him to enter, making crystal-clear meanwhile all that is involved, drawing him by the cords of love and sympathetic interest, but leaving him free finally either to come in or else to turn aside into the way which is broad and well-traveled and leads to destruction. Of all the tasks which the church, and the church alone, can perform in education, this is the hardest to put into words, and by all odds the most essential.

In the fourth place, the church has the distinctive responsibility of providing inspiration and guidance to the home in performing its work of Christian nurture. The emphasis upon the home is as old as Christianity itself, and indeed extends back into Jewish history. The trouble is that we have paid extravagant lip service to the centrality of the home, and that is about all!

Almost a decade ago the International Council of Religious Education released a basic document entitled *Christian Education Today*, in which this significant sentence occurred: "In view of the important place of the family in any comprehensive plan for Christian education, the establishing and sustaining of Christian families will itself become one of the goals toward which the efforts of Christian education will be directed."[3] The words are true and well said, but during the intervening years we have been busy with a multiplicity of interests and never seriously got around to putting them into effect. Now the Study Committee of the International Council none too gently takes us to task for our failure in this regard, and states in effect that we must either stop saying such things or else do something about them. Its major recommendation at this point is worded as follows: "That the International Council of Religious Education examine its present and prospective program, its literature, and its structure to discover the degree to which home religion receives the attention which it deserves, and that it then revise its program, processes, and structure so that the pre-eminence given to the family in its statements of basic philosophy is apparent in the full round of Council activities."[4] For all its polite diction, that recommendation has point and punch to it; and it is high time we began doing what it says we ought to do.

For family life has been falling apart in a manner approaching a debacle. The alarming divorce rate, which in many areas is one-third or one-half the marriage rate, is only a prominent symptom of a basic illness. In its nature the illness, as is so often the case, is a complication of diseases.

We are prone nowadays to blame everything on the war, and beyond a doubt it must carry its share of the burden. The war uprooted families from the stable soil in which they had been growing — churches, and neighbors, and community attachments. The war got many a new family off to a bad start, with a hasty and perhaps romantic and ill-considered marriage, a hurried honeymoon, and then long alienation in different modes of life on different continents. The net result is not merely the disruption of numerous present-day homes, but also the distortion of the mental patterns of the homemakers of tomorrow. Whether we like it or not, many of our children and youth have no stabilizing recollection of normal, happy home life. The full domestic toll of the war will not be apparent for five, or ten, or twenty years. Yes, the war has done its share; but the trouble was upon us long before the war began. We must probe deeper to find the full cause of the ailment.

As has been pointed out again and again, the changing circumstances of family life may be partly to blame. The modern city home is in many respects a far cry from the old homestead of a few generations ago. The ample house with its yard and garden have given way to an apartment poised precariously midway between earth and sky and constituted of a kitchenette, a dinette, a combination living room and bedroom, and a balcony. The several members of the family work in different places, play at different pursuits, and spend their leisure time with different sets of strangers. The canning is done in a cannery; the baking in a bakery; the washing in a laundry. In more ways than we can possibly outline here, the home is less of a home than it used to be. This portrait is, of course, part caricature; but it is also partly true, and in a measure is responsible for the low estate to which family life has fallen.

But even this does not take us to the root of the disease. Some careful observers have a more searching diagnosis. They say that at long last the selfish individualism of American life has invaded the citadel of the home, whose defenses held out longer than any other institution but succumbed at last to the insistent pressure. Now, they say, we are beginning to act in the home precisely the way we have acted outside the home for many years. That is, each individual is out to get all he can for himself. A boy and a girl marry for what they can get out of it, rather than what they can put into it. They seek quick returns of pleasure here as everywhere else; and if these are not forthcoming and up to expectations, they do not hesitate to call the whole thing off. The children, too, are motivated by the same spirit. They think more of rights than they do of responsibilities; more of selfish satisfaction than they do of sacrifice. And no institution has ever been able to hold together under such motivations.

Whatever be the explanation of the illness, concerning the illness itself there can be no question. The American home is sick, and needs a physician. This conviction has been growing upon us steadily. Coupled closely with it is another conviction, and these two taken together account for the new emphasis upon the home among the leaders of Christian education.

A realistic understanding of the dynamics of personality growth has finally dawned upon us, and has convinced us completely that the home is the place par excellence for the making or the marring of the human spirit. If the home is good, the personality results will normally be good. And if the home is bad, as it is today in many instances, the personality consequences are nothing short of catastrophic. For the home is the place where the real business of Christian nurture is transacted. It is perhaps the primary sacramental channel through which the grace of God would fain get at each growing life. What goes on within the walls of the church is important, but not sufficient. An hour or two hours a week, no matter how vital they may be, cannot turn the trick. It is the home which counts above all else.

The logic of the matter comes down at last to this: nothing short of religion can finally save the family, and nothing but the family can finally save religion. It is no wonder that a new concern for family life and family religion is manifest within the circles of Christian education.

One of the strongest sections of the report of the International Council's Study Committee deals with this subject. Embodied within it at various points are fascinating and reassuring glimpses of a new type of curriculum, which Boards of Christian Education will slowly translate into reality — a home-church curriculum. This is a daring new conception. Hitherto we have talked of a church curriculum, or a church school curriculum. But now we are beginning to speak of a home-church curriculum, a hyphenated affair, one part of which is to be administered in the church and another equally important part in the home, with the two aiding and abetting each other at every point.

The church part will run along somewhat familiar lines. The home part is largely a disembodied vision as yet. We think that it will include study materials to be pursued interestingly within the home, a sort of "homework" paralleling the church curriculum week by week. It should contain worship materials for the home, in which father and mother and children will find guidance and substance for their approach to God as a family group around a family altar. There may well be practical suggestions for the enrichment of family fellowship — games, songs, picnics, trips, and hobbies to be performed together. Perhaps there will be specific help on making the most of the red-letter days in the life of the family — Christmas, Easter, Hallowe'en, Thanksgiving, birthdays, baptism, confirmation, the lighting of a fire in the fireplace, and a trip to see grandmother and grandfather. This home curriculum ought to list attractively some good books for reading in the home, some good pictures to adorn the walls of the home, and some good music wherewith to make a joyful noise unto the Lord. Certainly it should not omit occasional sections for parents only, embodying the best findings of child and adolescent psychology so phrased that the ordinary father and mother will find them interesting and valuable. Here is a challenge for editors and curriculum-builders, the like of which has not appeared for a quarter of a century. And, in a larger sense, the challenge extends to us all to place the home at the center of our concept of Christian education, and to act accordingly.

We have said that this important educative task belongs peculiarly to the church. Surely no public school or social service agency can undertake it fully. They can help, and we shall need all the help we can get. But our responsibility as a church cannot be side-stepped. We must help the homes which encircle our churches to be what God has designed them to be, "ecclesiolae," little churches, miniature assemblies of the faithful, in which God will be truly worshiped and served, and life will become sacred and beautiful, and children will be reared in the nurture and admonition of the Lord.

Finally, the church has the distinctive educational task of preparing men and women for Christian leadership in every significant sphere of society. The training of leaders is, of course, the joint obligation of church, school, home, and community. But the training of Christian leaders, men and women whose professional equipment is interfused with Christian motivations and Christian ideals — that is the business of the church.

We said in an earlier discussion that the recovery of religion within general education waits upon public school teachers and professors who are competent and eager to draw out the proper religious implications of a subject whenever the opportunity presents itself. If our schools and colleges are to have teachers of this sort, who will also regard their vocation as a high calling of God to be followed in the spirit of Christian service and in accordance with Christian standards, the church must provide them.

One of the regrettable situations to be seen in our major communities is that social work, which was mothered in the first instance by the church, has strayed so far from home. All of us who have had any experience with social agencies know that quite a few of their workers have little religious faith of their own, and little respect for religious institutions. If our community agencies are to have case workers who are imbued with the Christian spirit, co-operative with the Christian church, and fully equipped to use the resources of Christianity in healing the wounds of individual and society, the church must provide them.

Many long-time friends of labor are deeply concerned over the recent trend of events within the labor movement. We are beginning to wonder whether we may not be on the edge of another era of irresponsible power, which is always bad no matter who exercises it. But if this is the case, we have only ourselves to blame in considerable part. In the degree to which the church has been a middle-class institution, failing to welcome laborers to our fellowship and failing to sympathize with the just aspirations of the laboring classes, we have made the labor movement what it is today. If the unions are to have Christian leaders, the church must provide them.

And we need not go so far as the Oxford Movement, in the hope that the conversion of a few industrialists will right our economic wrongs, to see that precisely the same truth prevails on the side of ownership and management. And in politics! And in international affairs! I believe we have all been grateful to know that John Foster Dulles was sitting with the statesmen of the world at San Francisco and in Moscow. If there are to be more like him, exercising leadership to the best of their ability in the Christian manner wherever major issues are being considered and the destinies of human beings decided, the church will have to provide them.

The question of just how this is to be done is another matter. It seems clear that more is required than the mere general teaching of broad Christian truth, important as that is. We may have to devise improved techniques for the application of Christian teaching to specific vocational categories, working out in some detail what it means to be a

Christian in the teaching profession, in business, in politics, and the like. We could probably do worse than to take a leaf from the Quaker book and begin gathering men and women together by vocational groups — lawyers in one, doctors in another, teachers in a third, and so on — for the purpose of exploring the depths of Christian meaning for each separate profession or calling.

Perhaps the most suitable closing note for this study and the entire series is to stress once again, as has been done so often in so many connections, the fact that the minister occupies a key position in Christian education at every point along the line. The election of Mr. Charles Taft, a layman, to the presidency of the Federal Council of the Churches of Christ in America has been the occasion for a good many observations on the importance of laymen in the Christian enterprise. This is undoubtedly true, and especially true in Protestantism. But the fact still remains that in the average congregation the minister is the only person professionally trained for Christian leadership. He is the only one whose time is completely set aside for the work of the church. He normally enjoys a considerable measure of prestige, so that what he regards as worth while others will regard as worth while, and what he works at others will work at. This all adds up, no more and no less, to the old saying, "Like priest, like people." It follows that a better day in religious education depends largely upon the ministers of our churches.

For the minister to busy himself with religious nurture involves no departure from the historic role of the ministry. Our Lord Himself was a teacher. We can aspire to nothing higher than to be like Him, in this respect as well as others.

NOTES)~

CHAPTER I

1. L. P. Jacks, *A Living Universe* (1924), p. 14. Used by permission of Harper & Brothers, Publishers.

2. George A. Buttrick, in *Association of American Colleges BULLETIN*, March, 1947, p. 38. Used by permission.

3. Paul H. Vieth, *The Church and Christian Education* (The Bethany Press, 1947), pp. 55-56. Used by permission.

CHAPTER II

1. Prepared by the U. S. Office of Education, and published in *The Messenger*, April 17, 1941, p. 22.

2. M. C. Miller, *Teaching the Multitudes* (The Beacon Publishers, 1944), p. 4.

3. *Ibid.*, pp. 56-57.

4. Quoted in *Teaching Religion in the Public School* by C. A. Hauser (1942), p. 84. By permission.

5. *International Journal of Religious Education*, June, 1944, p. 13.

6. Federal Council of the Churches of Christ in America.

7. *Ibid.*

8. *Ibid.*

9. *Ibid.*

10. *Ibid.*

11. *Religious Education*, April-June, 1940, pp. 72, 73.

12. Harrison S. Elliott, in *International Journal of Religious Education*, November, 1940, p. 40. Used by permission.

13. *Religious Education*, April-June, 1940, p. 73.

14. Paul H. Vieth, *The Church and Christian Education* (The Bethany Press, 1947), p. 302. Used by permission.

15. J. Paul Williams, in *The Christian Century*, March 12, 1947, p. 331. Reprinted by permission.

CHAPTER III

1. 1947 *Yearbook* of the International Council of Religious Education, p. 76.

2. Paul H. Vieth, *The Church and Christian Education* (The Bethany Press, 1947), p. 39.

3. M. C. Miller, *Teaching the Multitudes* (The Beacon Publishers, 1944), p. 209.

4. *Ibid.,* p. 211.

5. *Religious Education,* September-October, 1942, pp. 287, 289.

6. C. A. Hauser, *Latent Religious Resources in Public School Education* (The Heidelberg Press, 1924).

7. J. K. Beckes, *Interfaith Attitudes in Weekday Religious Education.* Abstracted in *Religious Education,* March-April, 1947, p. 105.

8. *International Journal of Religious Education,* June, 1948, pp. 4 ff.

9. C. H. Moehlman, *School and Church: The American Way* (Harper & Brothers, 1944), pp. 67-68.

10. *Ibid.,* pp. 75, 79.

11. See, for example, *The Christian Century,* February 26, 1947, pp. 262 ff.

12. *Religious Education,* March-April, 1947, p. 98.

CHAPTER IV

1. M. C. Miller, *Teaching the Multitudes* (The Beacon Publishers, 1944), p. 13.

2. Paul H. Vieth, *The Church and Christian Education* (The Bethany Press, 1947), pp. 146-147. Used by permission.

3. Quoted from *Christian Education Today,* copyrighted 1940 by the International Council of Religious Education, 203 N. Wabash Ave., Chicago 1, Ill. Used by permission.

4. Paul H. Vieth, *The Church and Christian Education* (The Bethany Press, 1947), pp. 186-187. Used by permission.

APPENDIX

The following Appendix, "The Relation of Religion to Public Education: The Basic Principles," is one of a series of Reports of Committees and Conferences of the American Council on Education, and is reprinted here with their kind permission.

AMERICAN COUNCIL ON EDUCATION STUDIES

The
Relation of Religion
TO
Public Education

The Basic Principles

By the COMMITTEE ON RELIGION AND EDUCATION

AMERICAN COUNCIL ON EDUCATION STUDIES

Series I

Reports of Committees and Conferences

THE RELATION OF RELIGION TO PUBLIC EDUCATION: THE BASIC PRINCIPLES is the first publication of the Committee on Religion and Education appointed by the American Council on Education in the spring of 1944. *Religion and Public Education* was the report of a conference held in Princeton, New Jersey, in May 1944, which led to the formation of the Committee to study the problems further.

FOREWORD ⟩∿

IN THE SPRING of 1944, the American Council on Education, with the co-operation of the National Conference of Christians and Jews, assembled a group of educators at Princeton, N. J., to discuss the relation of religion to public education. The conference included unofficial representatives of education on the elementary, secondary, and higher levels, under both public and private auspices, and leaders of the three major faiths in the United States. The purpose of the meeting was to exchange views on a matter of increasing concern to educators as well as to religious leaders and a considerable part of the lay public.

Following this meeting, which confined itself to its task of exploration and recommended no specific policy or program, the American Council created the Committee on Religion and Education to conduct or instigate such studies and educational activities in this area as might stimulate informed thinking. The committee undertook as its first task the preparation of the document here presented. The first purpose of the committee was to identify and define the issues that arise in considering the relationship between religion and public education in America in the light both of our educational history and of the total cultural pattern. It then undertook to analyze the existing situation and to state some broad principles which it is hoped will find a large measure of acceptance and which will stimulate constructive criticism and experimentation.

It should be emphasized that while the subject of the relation of religion to education in the philosophical sense is a very old one, there has been no general agreement concerning how this matter of fundamental importance should be treated in American public education. This report should, therefore, be regarded as a first step in a program of studies and experimental activities which I trust may be developed under the auspices of the committee.

GEORGE F. ZOOK
President

November 29, 1946

INTRODUCTION ↝

THAT THE PRESENT period is marked by an increased interest in religion perhaps goes without saying. It is evidenced in books, magazines, newspaper editorials and columns, on the stage and screen, and in less tangible ways. This growing interest is attested in education by the rapid spread of the weekday religious education movement, by the widely reported mood of seriousness with respect to religion on college campuses, and by increased discussion in educational circles of the responsibility of school and college in the field of religion. No great "revival of religion" is in evidence, but there is a "stirring of the waters."

These signs of awakened interest in religion are variously appraised. By some they are thought to be only temporary and due to the stress and strain incident to economic depression and war. There are others who believe that this interest springs from a desire to escape the rigorous requirements of living in a time of crisis and hardship. It is well to keep in mind that not every form in which a religious mood expresses itself is wholesome or indicative of an abiding attitude. But those who believe that religion is fundamental in man's life will not be deterred by manifest crudities of expression from seeing the significance of an appeal in time of crisis to the ultimate sources of faith, courage, and hope. No more authentic note has been sounded in the record of human experience than this: "Out of the depths have I cried unto thee . . ."!

Certainly the intensified religious concern that is manifest today demands attention by educators. It is part of the complex situation with which education must deal. This is not to say that every particular popular demand must be accepted. Educators may not abdicate their responsibility for leadership in educational matters; this fact often requires resistance to a popular mood for such time as may be required for thinking through a complicated question in democratic fashion. But even if it be assumed that existing conceptions and policies with reference to religion and education call for no changes whatever, that position cannot rest merely on affirmation; it must be supported by fresh reasoning in the light of a changing situation.

It is highly proper, therefore, that all proposals for teaching religion in the schools should be closely scrutinized, for no innovations should come about without benefit of thoughtful criticism. It may well be argued that many proposals for bridging the gap between religion and education are ill-considered and fraught with danger. However, if untenable proposals are here and there advanced and adopted in the field of religious education, they may be in fact a result of an educational policy that has tended to isolate religion from other phases of community life. Nothing elemental in human life can be indefinitely isolated in this fashion. It comes back to protest in unexpected ways. This is happening today in the religious field.

It is urged that educators, and also the lay public with whom the determination of educational policy ultimately rests in a democracy, approach this problem as objectively as the committee tried to do in order that sound judgments may be reached. There is need for the most thorough presentation of every point of view provided it is seriously held and factually supported. Much writing and speaking have rested on assumptions with reference to the existing situation that run counter to ascertainable facts. Prejudice has not been lacking in presenting either pros or cons. The committee has tried to say nothing in this report about which it is not ready to hear criticism with the same respect that is bespoken for its own judgments.

In preparing this report many sources have been drawn upon, but few citations are given because it is earnestly desired that the judgments expressed shall be weighed on their merits, dissociated from particular controversial discussions and special pleadings.

In such a report as is here presented, it is not to be assumed that every sentence or phrase is in the form that each member of the committee would have chosen. Yet it records essential agreement upon a document that represents a genuinely co-operative effort.

CONTENTS ⟩⟨

CHAPTER I

THE SECULARIZATION
OF MODERN LIFE

THE SECULAR character of our public educational system cannot be understood without reference to the secularization of life in the Western world. The influence upon our culture of the Judaeo-Christian tradition has been profound; in large measure it has given us our system of values. But in modern times the values originally associated with religion have been largely dissociated from religious sanctions. Religion continues to evidence itself in fundamental beliefs, in a mood of reverence, and in specifically religious observances. Yet religion has largely lost its significance for many areas of human activity. Politics, business and industry, and the broad patterns of group behavior are no longer responsive to definite religious sanctions, however much the forms of religion continue to receive traditional respect. This is the expression of secularism in recent history, not a denial of religion, but the denial of its relevance to the major activities of life.

There is another and more extreme sense of the term "secularism" which denotes a definite philosophy of life which has no place for religious creeds or for the institutions of worship. Some of those who write currently in defense of secularism are advocating a philosophy that is a substitute for religion. This is something quite different from the historical development of gradual dissociation between the imperatives of religion and the demands of the world. They appear to regard secularism as a complete way of life, thus implying that it is an ethical philosophy by which one may live and a philosophy which rejects religion in all its historical forms.

We reject secularism as a philosophy of life and we cannot agree that it has ever been accepted as such by the American people. Those who do adopt it tend to make it, in effect, a rival religion and to insist with unwitting inconsistency that it become the basis of American education. On the other hand, we recognize as historical fact the secularization of life and education, finding the real significance of that term in the separation of religion from the rest of life. This secularization of life as a modern phenomenon does not imply an intention to destroy religious faith or religious institutions, but rather to isolate them from politics, business, and education. But it is our contention that although secularization in this sense involves no such negative philosophic assumptions as some current writers find in it, it does tend inevitably toward the eclipse of religion by ignoring it as an essential part of the culture and rendering it innocuous. In particular, the secularization of education tends *in actual practice* to outrun the original intention it expressed. We are convinced that the vast majority of the American people, to whom the schools belong, would repudiate the assumption that secularization of the schools expresses an intentional devaluation of religious faith or religious institutions. But how many of them see the ultimate *implications* of secularization is another matter. It has been supported as an educational policy as vigorously by some churchmen as by persons outside the church.

Further confusion results from the fact that the word "secularization" is often used in relation to the general subject of this report as denoting the separation of education from church control. We shall have something to say later concerning the church-state problem, but at this point it should be noted that the divorce of public education from ecclesiastical control, which is an accepted American policy, is not synonymous with the separation of religion from education. The fact that our population is religiously heterogeneous puts the separation of church and state, as a broad political principle, beyond debate, regardless of what theories may be held concerning what would be appropriate in a different kind of society.

Let us now consider the origin of the secularization of life as a historical movement which antedates by a long period the secularization of American education. No single explanation of the beginning of the secularist trend can be given. The causes of historical changes are always multiple. Cultural forces of great magnitude have long been at work in the Western world.

The history of Europe in the Middle Ages is in great part the history of the Christian church. Christianity furnished the central framework of ideas and values about which medieval society was built. The bond which united the Western world was primarily religious, not political. Such unity as was attained was an ecclesiastical achievement. In the late Middle Ages there obtained what has been called the "medieval synthesis" — a weaving together of philosophy, theology, and individual and social ethics in a comprehensive Christian system of thought and life. This is not to say that this system was always observed as a discipline. As is true today, ethical principles were sometimes more honored in the breach than in the observance. But they were *honored*. There was general acceptance of common spiritual sanctions which included the social, political, and economic spheres of activity as well as that of private, personal relationships. There was an "ethic" of group relationships that was integrated with the code of personal morals.

The conception of universal moral law which underlies the modern system of common law, the body of reciprocal rights and duties which gave stability to feudal society, the principle of representative government which the Middle Ages bequeathed to the modern world, and that extraordinarily inclusive system of social ethics which gave unity and coherence to the common life — these are among the achievements for which the church must be given chief credit. They are cited here not to foster nostalgia for the Middle Ages, but to indicate the background against which modern secularism must be viewed. However much it may suffer by comparison with the modern era, medieval Europe had a framework of spiritual unity which the modern world conspicuously lacks. It should be possible to learn from the past without returning to it.

This unity and coherence of thought and life disappeared with the fragmentizing of the Western world politically and religiously. The scope of religious sanctions was gradually narrowed, and significant areas of the common life of men acquired an autonomy of their own. In particular, the economic sphere began to take on an aspect of self-containment. The concept of "economic man" and the contemporary slogan "business is business" are expressions of the changed outlook. Such notions would have been well-nigh meaningless to the men of the Middle Ages. They strikingly illustrate the secularist trend.

The rise of the middle class operated to shift the locus of power to competing economic groups, and later to foster the conception of economic processes as automatic. In the course of time the notion that economic controls normally resided in the "mechanisms of the market" came to be dominant, completing the secularization of the economic sphere. This development is a major concern to many students of the culture who see in it the divorce of essential areas of the common life from the religious sanctions that were once acknowledged as applicable to all conduct. The struggle in modern education to gain a secure place for the study of controversial issues has arisen in considerable part from this self-sufficiency of the economic sphere. The right of the schools to scrutinize the social order has been challenged largely because the economic structure of society has been held to be self-justifying and immune to criticism. To say this involves no judgment with reference to particular economic theories. The point is rather that the tendency to regard the economic order as outside the proper sphere of moral criticism, whether in school or church, is a secularist phenomenon of prime importance.

By a curious anomaly, religion itself has contributed to this situation. The *laissez faire* philosophy was originally in large part an expression of belief about the way God rules the world. It was maintained that the automatic operation of the market was a divinely ordained instrumentality for securing the maximum social good through the interplay of individual efforts directed by self-interest. The economic order was presided over by an "absentee God." It seems probable that the idea was a grand rationalization in support of a cultural movement that had acquired a vast momentum. This conception of God has been outmoded, but the *laissez faire* idea dies hard. The contemporary effort of the major religious groups in America, as in other industrialized countries, to develop criteria for evaluating and criticizing the forms of economic life is an emphatic protest against this tendency to make the economic system a self-sufficient mechanism.

We have stressed the economic aspect of this subject because it is perhaps the most conspicuous example of the secularist view according to which one phase of the culture can properly remain immune from the ethical impact of religion. The same inhibition has been evident in other phases of the culture, including practically every aspect of the general welfare which requires political action for its defense and improvement. It is a matter of common observation that attempts on the part of the pulpit to influence political action, even in entirely nonpartisan fashion, have called forth admonitions to "stick to the gospel." It is the essence of secularism to render religion innocuous by isolating it from practical affairs.

Happily, this resistance is yielding to moral pressure, and organized religion is again speaking with a greater measure of prophetic effectiveness. In the Protestant churches a vigorous antisecularist movement has gone by the name of the "social gospel." The Catholic church has long striven toward an organic conception of society, in which functional groups and social instrumentalities would operate under a unitary moral law. Judaism has sought to re-establish throughout the social order the broad concept of social justice, as proclaimed by the prophets of Israel and developed by the later Jewish sages. All these are manifestations of opposition to the modern trend toward separation of the religious from the secular.

Another major factor in the secularization of life is the growth of the modern scientific movement which at its inception revolutionized man's view of his world. It should go without saying that we wish to give no support to antiscientific notions or movements. The scientific method itself has a profoundly moral aspect. It is a symptom of secularism, however, that the scientific sphere of activity should have claimed and so largely secured for itself an autonomy of its own. The struggle going on within the scientific fraternity over the relation of science to values bears eloquent testimony to the dualism that has come to characterize modern life — an artificial separation between what may be called the things of the mind and the things of the spirit. The current effort on the part of socially minded scientists to make science the servant of values would seem to be a sound application of the instrumentalist principle which has received so much emphasis in recent philosophical writing.

The function of science, as such, is to study the phenomenal world and to render it intelligible to a maximum degree. It is concerned with phenomena about which persons of equal competence and equipped with equivalent apparatus can validate each other's findings. But the ultimate nature of reality is something about which scientists in the same field and of equal competence differ, and presumably will continue to differ. This is inevitable because ultimate reality is the concern, not of science, but of philosophy and religion. Some of our greatest scientists are philosophical agnostics because they find no guidance in their respective disciplines concerning the nature of reality. Others of equivalent standing in their fields hold to historical religious beliefs.

Here again, however, it must be recognized that many persons have in the name of religion contributed to an obscurantist, antiscientific view of life by false claims to authority in the scientific sphere. If science is not a substitute for religion, neither can religion be a substitute for science. It is not the province of religion to make pronouncements in the field of biology or geology. The long history of conflict between science and theology is a melancholy record of obstruction to the free play of intelligence in both the scientific and the religious spheres. It has hampered religion as well as science. Happily, the error underlying this obstructionist attitude is coming to be recognized by religious leaders in all the major faith groups, each of which has contributed notably to leadership in scientific inquiry, experimentation, and discovery. But if there is no warrant for hostility to science on the part of religion, it is equally true that science can offer no substitute for religious faith.

CHAPTER II

THE SECULARIZATION
OF EDUCATION
AND ITS CONSEQUENCES

THE FOREGOING discussion of the secularist mood and outlook that characterize our time has seemed necessary as a background for consideration of the secularization of education. The latter phenomenon could hardly have come about without the former, for in an important sense it is all of a piece with the secularization of the culture. The changing world-outlook and the development of an autonomous economic system within an autonomous political order created an intellectual and moral environment in which the secularization of education could take place with a minimum of resistance.

Yet we think it a cardinal error to assume that the extreme degree of secularization which has come about in many of our school systems — by no means all of them — was an inevitable consequence of the forces whose operations we have been considering. Competent researches show the contrary. The immediate cause of the exclusion of religious teaching from the schools was sectarian conflict.

It is well known that prior to the establishment of our public school system, the church played a dominant role in education. Indeed, the church has been called the mother of the school. American educational history is in this respect largely a projection of the European tradition in its Protestant forms. It was Puritan New England, where the government took a theocratic form, that bequeathed to the nation its system of publicly con-

trolled schools. This pattern developed early in New England because its component states were so largely of one faith that the
community tended to reflect and perpetuate the religious tradition
which had been dominant from early colonial times. This religious unity resulted in no small part from religious intolerance
which had made life uncomfortable for dissident groups. The
net result, however, was to furnish a congenial climate for the
development of community-controlled education. The ensuing
struggle over religious teaching in the schools was a contest over
sectarianism, not over the importance of religion in education.

We may, therefore, dismiss the notion that the American
people set about deliberately to eliminate religion from education.
For a variety of reasons they gradually came to accept the principle of publicly controlled education, maintained by public
funds, and to exclude church control over public education as a
matter of policy. This, of course, did not mean the elimination
of private and parochial schools. Having accepted this principle,
the American people felt driven to the conclusion that if religious
teaching could not be carried on in the public schools without
sectarian strife it would have to go. In part, the reluctance with
which this decision was reached was tempered by the hope that
the rising Sunday school movement would supply what was lacking in the public schools. The responsibility for the condition
that made the decision inevitable must rest heavily on the religious community itself.

Horace Mann, secretary of the Massachusetts State Board of
Education, 1837-48, who bore the brunt of the battle over the
exclusion from the schools of sectarian religious teaching, enter-
tained the hope that a way would be found to foster religious
faith in a nonsectarian and therefore generally acceptable fashion.
His overwhelming concern was with the chaos which he saw in
the religious situation. Making due allowance for a certain ex-

travagance of statement, one finds some of his comments highly illuminating. When he looked for textbooks in which some common faith was expressed, he found none that were "free from the advocacy of particular 'tenets' and 'sects.'" The proposal that each town or school district should determine what doctrine should be taught called forth this scornful rejoinder: "It is easy to see that the experiment would not stop with having half a dozen conflicting creeds taught by authority of law, in the different schools of the same town or vicinity. Majorities will change in the same place. One sect may have the ascendancy today; another, tomorrow. . . . This year, the everlasting fires of hell will burn, to terrify the impenitent; next year, and without any repentance, its eternal flames will be extinguished — to be rekindled forever, or to be quenched forever, as it may be decided at annual town meetings. This year, under Congregational rule, the Rev. Mr. So and So, and the Rev. Dr. So and So, will be on the committee; but next year, these Reverends and Reverend Doctors will be plain Misters — never having had apostolical consecration from the Bishop. This year, the ordinance of baptism is inefficacious without immersion; next year one drop of water will be as good as forty fathoms."[1]

Mann actually favored religious instruction in the schools to the fullest extent possible "without invading those rights of conscience which are established by the laws of God and guaranteed to us by the Constitution of the State."[2] He once wrote, "Entirely to discard the inculcation of the great doctrines of morality and of natural theology has a vehement tendency to drive mankind into opposite extremes; to make them devotees on one side, or profligates on the other; each about equally regardless of the

1. Raymond B. Culver, *Horace Mann and Religion in the Massachusetts Public Schools* (New Haven: Yale University Press, 1929), p. 208.

2. *Ibid.*, p. 207.

true constituents of human welfare. Against a tendency to these fatal extremes, the beautiful and sublime truths of ethics and of natural religion have a poising power."[3]

The hope of Horace Mann that a body of commonly accepted religious beliefs might be taught in the schools was not realized. Many entertain that hope today. There are reasons, however, for regarding such a proposal as of doubtful wisdom and equally doubtful feasibility. The point to be stressed is that the *intent* of the movement which Mann led was not to exclude all religious subject matter from the educative process as carried on under public auspices. Yet he saw no way to avoid it, and he was ready, apparently, to accept the policy which actually led to that result if that was the only way to keep the schools free from religious controversy. How much he would have deplored the ultimate consequence can readily be imagined.

The assumption that a school system from which all study of religion should be excluded was what the American people really wanted when they secularized education runs counter not only to our educational, but to our religious, history. Contrary to what seems to be a common assumption, organized religion was much less strong at the time the Republic was founded than at the time when the struggle over religion in the schools was at its height. It is estimated that at the end of the colonial period not more than five percent of the population were active church members. The percentage almost trebled in the next fifty years. These facts do not invalidate our generalizations about the secularization of the culture, for church membership is not an index of the influence of religion upon the social order. The facts do, however, make it difficult to regard the exclusion of religion from the schools as a direct expression of flagging interest in religion as such. Our purpose here is to correct the impression that the di-

---

3. *Ibid.*, p. 42.

vorce of education from religion was what was desired when sectarian teaching was banished from the schools.

Thus, it appears that while the secularization of education took its place historically as an aspect of a long-term cultural trend, it has quite outrun the intention of those educational leaders who initiated the movement. In so doing, it probably reinforced the general secularist trend in America. May it be supposed that any interest or concern that does not find active expression in the public schools can hold a permanent place in the public mind? We are not suggesting that all education of the young must take place in school. Obviously, the school is not the only educator. The home is probably most influential in putting a stamp upon the characters of children and giving them an outlook on life. Organized recreation is also a great educator. But these extra-school agencies are not, and should not be, expected to pre-empt an educational area from which thereafter the school remains aloof. On the contrary, the importance of the home and of organized play impel the school to give increasing attention to education for family life and to extraschool recreational activities. To leave religious education entirely to church and synagogue is in contrast to educational policy in other matters. To do this is to invite the same indifference to religion that we should expect to result in the political sphere from ignoring the institutions of government. This is not to anticipate the consideration of problems and difficulties that we have yet to explore, but only to ask that the presumable effect upon the religious life of the community of continually ignoring religion in the public schools be faced frankly.

Also, we emphasize the fact that this dualism in education cuts directly across the trend in modern educational theory and practice toward identifying school and community. However many or diverse the instrumentalities for education may be, the public school is increasingly regarded as a unifying agency. To have avoided sectarian teaching in the public schools was a real and necessary achievement, but to perpetuate in education a dualism in our culture is another matter. As time passes, the inconsistency of excluding the study of religion becomes more, rather than less, marked. The school itself is emphasizing a division, a split, in the educative process which its own philosophy increasingly repudiates. To avoid this contradiction one must either accept the patent inference that religious education is relatively unimportant and a marginal interest, or assume that religion is a matter so remote from life that it admits of no integration with the general educational program.

CHAPTER III

WHAT WE MEAN BY RELIGION

WHENEVER the subject we have here under discussion is broached the question arises: What is meant by religion? The very raising of the question is significant in two respects.

First, it is characteristic of a secular age that people should have no clear understanding of what religion means. We have noted the tendency of secularization to foster a denial of the relevance of religion to politics, business, and other practical affairs. When the common life is so largely divorced from the sanctions of the religious-ethical tradition, with the result that an artificial split occurs in the culture between the religious and the secular, religion tends to become "a private idiosyncrasy." Had this isolation of religion not occurred, the question, What is religion? would not be raised so often.

Secondly, we hold that inability to agree on a definition of religion should not deter any community from giving consideration to the place of religion in the school program. The fact that so many diverse ideas are held today concerning the nature and function of religion accentuates the importance of thoughtful study.

Nevertheless, it seems appropriate to indicate at this point what we think religion means in thought, feeling, and observance to the masses of the American people. Nothing that can be said in such brief space can be taken as adequate. Nor will any general statement made for the purposes of this discussion be what adherents of a particular faith would give voice to on their own account.

In simple terms religion implies an ultimate reality to which supreme allegiance must be given. To this ultimate reality men have from time immemorial given a name—God. The religious man finds warrant for all his conceptions of worth, of right, of duty, and of human destiny in his relationship to this ultimate reality. There is a wide difference in the ways in which men define this concept of God, ranging from highly personal to abstract philosophical terms; from emphasis on the transcendent to emphasis on the immanent; from a frankly supernatural conception to one that endows the cosmos itself with spiritual purpose and power. However, religion affirms overwhelmingly a reality that transcends the flux of events and constrains men toward the true and good.

On the subjective side religion commands men to respond to a divine imperative. It challenges them to an act of faith and to a commitment of the will. The extent to which religion is rational and the extent to which it is emotional are matters on which no agreement exists, but that it is profoundly volitional, calling for supreme personal commitment and loyalty, all are agreed. What one believes about God, about man, and about the world has momentous consequences in life and conduct.

But religion in human experience is by no means wholly accounted for in individualistic terms. It is also social and corporate. It expresses itself in institutions which organize themselves about the function of group worship. Here again there is great variety. There are highly elaborated rituals that have grown up in the more sacramentarian forms of religion, and there is the simple ritual of silence in which the worshipers feel themselves to be in the presence of God. The unifying principle is organized worship in which men seek to "make the Most High their habitation." In the churches and synagogues of America there is an extremely wide range of theological as well as ritualistic differences, but they have in common this principle of corporate worship.

It should be noted that throughout these pages religion is referred to as a phase of the culture because we believe the responsibility of public education with reference to religion is determined by fidelity to the culture in its entirety. In an important sense, however, religion is more than a *part* of the culture. A vital religious faith permeates every cultural good and influences every aspect of life. To those who take it seriously, religious faith is the spiritual foundation of society and indispensable to an enduring social structure. We believe that, in spite of the secularization of American life, the majority of our people are desirous that this foundation be greatly strengthened.

CHAPTER IV

WHAT WE MEAN
BY "TEACHING"

AT THIS POINT we would draw attention to what seems to us a basic difficulty in the solution of the problem we are facing. Twice during recent years the nature of the teaching and learning process has come in for intensive re-examination. First, with the development of the progressive education movement during the early part of this century, the traditional notion of education as imparting facts and indoctrinating with ideas was sharply challenged. The educative process came to be conceived as active rather than passive, as centering in the learner's felt needs and purposes, and as depending for its effectiveness on his own confirmatory response to what was presented to him, and its purposeful incorporation in his life. The slogan, "Not what to think, but how to think," became a common expression of the aim of education. It is not suggested that this movement has been influential throughout American education; on the contrary! But it has been highly influential in the great teacher-education centers and in educational literature. And it is probably safe to say that it has left a permanent deposit in the development of the American tradition. It has been vigorously attacked on the score of its alleged inadequacy in social discipline and in equipping the young with the knowledge and skills which the community has a right to expect in the product of its schools. However, the graduates of schools influenced by this philosophy have stood up well by comparison with those of traditional schools as measured by achievement at the college level, and have shown a high degree of social competence in the broad sense of that term. On the whole, they have made an impressive showing in ability to think for themselves about the significant problems of social living. If these schools have been, in many instances, defective in respect to the development of self-discipline, it is fair to say that efforts are being made to correct the fault.

However, a second re-examination of the teaching process was induced by the impact of the social, political, and moral crises of the last fifteen years, which confronted education with problems of a new sort. Some of them are outside the scope of this document, but the issue of indoctrination has been freshly raised in a way that is definitely related to the problem we are attempting to analyze. In recent years, many educators of the progressive type have raised serious questions about the formula "not what to think, but how to think." The crucial question has been whether or not the schools should be content to let boys and girls grow up to think what they like about democracy. The sharpening of what is loosely called ideological conflict has created anxiety among educators who had set great store by open-mindedness as an attitude to be fostered. It is scarcely possible to reconcile the recent crusading literature on education for democracy with the former insistence that definite "conditioning" was to be avoided. More and more it is coming to be demanded that the schools take sides in the battle between rival social philosophies and aim definitely at turning out young democrats.

This does not mean that the tide in public education is running in favor of indoctrination in the sense that a set of values or beliefs is to be presented to young minds for acceptance without question. Perhaps it would be more accurate to say that educators of the progressive type are engaged in reformulating their educational philosophy on this wise: To be educated does not mean to have been taught what to think, but it does mean to have learned what to think *about* and to have acquired definite convictions with respect to values. And the more realistic students of education recognize that however important freedom of thought may be in a liberal democratic culture, society inevitably demands that its schools equip the young with a lively appreciation of their cultural heritage and prepare them to carry forward the main stream of the culture. In this sense the schools are, in the nature of the case, custodians of the culture and the main instrumentality for its perpetuation. Hence, it would appear that the controversy about whether education is transmissive or critical is in some sense artificial. Education must be both. It must equip the young not only to *pass* on the culture but to pass *on* the culture. Only an appreciative understanding of tradition makes possible a critical appraisal of it.

This issue in educational philosophy has been highlighted in the battle over the social studies program, to which reference has been made. Socially minded educators have defended the introduction of controversial social and economic questions at the appropriate age level on the ground that the students need to know what the issues are, to be guided in their analysis of them in the light of the American tradition, and to have a sympathetic understanding of all honest proposals for their solution. In defending this position, they have no thought of indoctrination with one particular social philosophy. If they analyze for their students the issues of a political campaign, it is not for the purpose of instructing them as to how their parents should vote. At the same time, the very insistence on attention to fundamental issues constitutes pressure against a nonparticipating and neutral attitude. In such education there is an impulsive force toward action in the political arena. Indeed, all social education in the new pattern has this double character: it avoids partisanship on issues which divide the community, but it impels the citizen, young or old, to action upon conviction. Thus, he becomes the author of his own partisanship. To a considerable extent some religious schools have been following a similar course in the teaching of social ethics.

We have dwelt on this question concerning the nature of teaching in general because it is basic to a consideration of how the teaching of religion is to be understood. Strangely enough, whenever the possibility of introducing religious subject matter into the school program is suggested, it is inferred that what is proposed is a kind of indoctrination that has been increasingly disapproved in general educational practice. In the light of the foregoing discussion it appears that this inference is all of a piece with the resistance encountered in the social studies program. The place of religion in education is not easily defined, and many valid questions have been raised about it which require sober consideration. But we are impressed with the fact that the problem is usually misapprehended, even in otherwise thoughtful discussions of the subject. To assume that when religious subject matter is introduced into the schools the result is the adoption of a school theology is to beg the entire question. Here the same assumption is made that critics of the social studies have made when they have confused the study of economic problems with anticapitalist indoctrination.

That there have been efforts to introduce sectarian teaching in the school curriculum and that some current proposals look in that direction is not to be denied. We shall return in another connection to contemporary practices of this sort. Our purpose at this point is to urge consideration by educators of the possibility of raising the ban on religious subject matter to the extent that the study of it can be guided as is the case today in those schools which most successfully direct the study of other material about which divergent views are recognized. Such a procedure, however, rests on one positive assumption, namely, that among the results which the community has a right to look for in the graduates of its schools is a positive attitude toward the values that religion represents in the culture.

CHAPTER V

SHALL THE SCHOOLS TEACH A COMMON CORE OF RELIGIOUS BELIEF?

WE FULLY realize that the position just stated is at variance with the proposal currently put forward to abstract from the various faiths the common doctrines and make these the basis of religious instruction in the schools. This proposal is aimed at finding a nonsectarian basis for religious indoctrination. It requires serious scrutiny. To begin with, we think it objectionable from the religious point of view. Catholics, in particular, will object because of their traditional position that Christ established one true church to which all men are called. The notion of a common core suggests a watering-down of the several faiths to the point where common essentials appear. This might easily lead to a new sect — a public school sect — which would take its place alongside the existing faiths and compete with them. The great religious bodies in America hold their respective faiths too seriously to admit of such a procedure on the part of the public schools.

Furthermore, it must be remembered that not only are there many persons who are outside the churches and synagogues but also that there are those who are actively opposed to their teachings. They have their claim on the schools as well as others. To attempt the formulation of a common theology to be used as the basis of instruction in the sense of indoctrination would be bitterly resented by many persons, some of whom are teachers and others of whom are members of boards of education.

Finally, such a proposal runs counter to the trend in educational philosophy which we have already sketched. We do not believe the schools should be asked to do in the religious realm what they have rejected in other fields. Religious educators themselves are divided on whether or not intellectual conviction may be properly secured through indoctrination. This method has many defenders. Nevertheless, the contrary view has won its way in public education.

Here, however, a problem arises which we must face frankly. It may be contended that the disavowal of indoctrination in the school for any particular set of religious beliefs is fatal to our previously stated position that the school has a responsibility for fostering appreciation of the religious elements in the culture. If there are in the community which supports the schools those who reject religion *in toto,* who believe it anachronistic and a deterrent to progress, by what right, one may ask, shall the school undertake to foster an interest in it through the study of religious institutions? If, on the other hand, religion be given a place in the school program because of the conspicuous place it holds in the life of the community, how, it may be asked, would the democratic principle be violated by determining on a similar basis a minimum body of religious doctrine for which the school may stand?

The problem is fundamental. We have noted the tendency in educational practice to substitute guided inquiry for the proclamation of doctrine and, on the other hand, the newer tendency to fix in the minds of the young a set of values and attitudes with reference to the democratic way of life. The latter is insisted upon despite the fact that there are persons in the community who do not subscribe to the creed of democracy in any fundamental sense. For example, the schools are permitted to foster the concept of equality in spite of the fact that the principle of equality is notoriously violated in more than one phase of our national life. Admittedly, to force this principle upon some sections of the population would be to incur the danger of violence. Indeed, it may be plausibly maintained that there are more people in America who believe in God than there are people who believe in democracy as a way of life! There is much evidence to support that contention. But democracy is part of our cultural heritage, and in spite of all our denials of it we feel committed to the democratic ideal. So it is with our religious heritage. We who make this report believe that the American people are deeply, though not always articulately, conscious of a religious heritage to whose central values they want their children to be committed. We believe this is the reason for the renewed widespread concern for education in the field of religion.

This is something quite different from a desire to impose some particular orthodoxy on the schools. The fact is that the scientific method has laid hold so firmly on the modern mind that the teaching of *any* doctrine as ultimately true and beyond question is resisted. The conviction is widespread that this kind of indoctrination can be justified only within groups whose members are so convinced of its finality as to be willing to fasten it on the minds of the young. It is noteworthy that even in churches which maintain the most rigid orthodoxy and which teach it in authoritarian fashion, the fact is recognized that belief cannot be coerced though it may be induced in a variety of ways. The American people as a whole are quite unwilling to accept the authority of the state to prescribe religious beliefs. It is safe to say that the continuing resistance to the introduction of religious matter into the schools is in large part due to the assumption that any such proposal really means the teaching of some particular religion — perhaps a synthetic one — as authoritative. If, in order to bring economics and political science into the schools through the social studies program it had been necessary to determine in advance "which economics to teach," the school program would have had to remain closed to that subject.

The substance of the matter is that contemporary society in America, placing a high value upon education, asks more and more of its schools in terms of curriculum scope and thoroughness, but distinctly less than formerly in terms of final pronouncements on anything. Until this characteristic of education in our time is fully appreciated, the situation must remain anomalous. There are those who think the school program has been too hospitable to newly developed fields of interest. To the modern-minded school administrator this complaint is likely to make little appeal, but it serves to emphasize the current trend. The criterion of acceptance in the curriculum is not universal agreement; rather it may be said that the presumption is in favor of inclusion in the school program of any area of interest that lends itself to objective study if a substantial portion of the constituency of the schools regards it as of vital concern. Educators have shown an impressive breadth of social vision in this respect. We suggest that a consistent adherence to the present-day philosophy of education and a responsible attitude toward their leadership function call for a new and serious approach on the part of educators to the problem of the place to be given to religion in the school program.

WILL TEACHING
"SPIRITUAL VALUES" SUFFICE?

AN IMPRESSIVE attempt has been made recently to demonstrate the essential adequacy of public education in moral and spiritual terms without the introduction of specifically religious subject matter. The point is of basic importance. We think the controversy over this subject has been needlessly sharpened by a tendency on the part of spokesmen for religion to condemn our schools indiscriminately because of the exclusion of religion. This exclusion is by no means universal, and there is abundant evidence that no general hostility to religion exists among educators. Large numbers of school superintendents and teachers are active and devoted laymen, representing all the major faiths. There is excellent reason to believe that nowhere is the concern over the exclusion of religion more deeply felt than within the educational profession. Large numbers of educators find it hard to accept some of the contemporary arguments for the traditional educational dualism — the separation of the religious from the secular.

Moreover, the defense of the public schools on the ground of the spiritual values they foster is wholly justified if they are being attacked on that score. We in America believe that democracy is a spiritual ideal; that co-operation, mutual aid, self-discipline, kindness, courtesy, and the like are spiritual values. The discipline of the scientific method has a definitely ethical quality. It requires fidelity to truth, the subordination of private motives, the suppression of bias, active co-operation with colleagues in the work of investigation, and, at its best, the making available of the results for public use.

Current attempts to defend the right of the public schools to develop spiritual values should not be necessary. We are not aware that the responsibility of the schools for fostering these ideals and developing corresponding attitudes is being challenged or that their achievements in these respects are being denied in any responsible quarter. If the schools are attacked on these grounds we heartily join in their defense. We would go farther and say that in many schools an attitude of religious reverence is fostered. Often, however, this is done in a hesitant and tentative way.

But to assume that spiritual values embody the full, valid content of religion is quite another matter. The words "spiritual" and "moral" denote the value-structure of life. Religion seeks personal identification with some ultimate source of values. It involves faith in the permanent validity and durability of these values. Religion has always supplied moral sanctions for men's actions. No person is fully educated who has not gained a knowledge of the faiths men live by. And unless the schools are content to leave one of the major areas of life unexplored, the specifically religious beliefs and aspirations of human beings must have attention.

This, however, is only a part of the matter. Religion is not only a faith to be believed but a life to be lived, which involves group as well as individual behavior. The man in the street knows that religion has something to do with church and synagogue. It is popular today to depreciate institutions. Yet without them, life would have no continuity and society would have no visible embodiment. Religion has, of course, its private and personal aspect, which is a precious possession. The right of the private conscience must be preserved. But, historically, religion has been profoundly social. It is associated with elemental needs of a social group. It expresses itself in ceremonial, in ritual and liturgy. Any adequate study of religion, therefore, includes the study of religious institutions.

In other fields of study this principle is clearly recognized. Educators long since discovered that economics could not be studied merely as a body of doctrine. It has been found necessary to include the story of corporations, banks, labor unions, trade associations, and co-operatives. The study of politics would be shallow indeed if it did not concern itself with the institutions of government and the actual functioning of political parties. It would not occur to anyone that because economic and political values are taught in the schools, the study of the institutions to which they give rise can be ignored. How can public education discharge its full obligation to interpret the culture if it excludes the study of religious institutions?

CHAPTER VII

EDUCATION THAT NEGATES RELIGION

AT THIS POINT we must give voice to a grievous concern on the part of many religious leaders and many educators as well. Much of the literature opposing any religious teaching in the schools has implicit in it, if not explicit, a definite philosophy that is, in effect, sectarian. And in many institutions of higher education and of teacher education, a system of philosophy is taught — in the traditional indoctrinational sense of that word — which negates the religious beliefs of millions of Americans. To present such a system of philosophy with the emphatic endorsement of the instructor while at the same time contending that religion must be kept out of public education is strangely inconsistent. For a naturalistic philosophy involves religious assumptions quite as much as a supernaturalistic philosophy. To call supernaturalism a religion and naturalism a philosophy and on that basis to exclude the one and embrace the other is, we think, a form of self-deception. Again, it should be emphasized that a supernaturalist world view is only partially representative of American religious philosophy. There are many religious leaders who find it unacceptable because they hold to a unitary view of all reality. But, to vast numbers of Americans, the denial of the supernatural in the classroom is a negation of their faith and to make such denial is to bring religion into the schools with a vengeance. If this unilateral exercise of "liberty" in a publicly supported institution is insisted on, only trouble can be expected. Religious people have every right to resent and resist an attack on their faith made in the name of academic scholarship.

There is a disquieting feeling abroad that the most grievous infraction of the American principle by which sectarian teaching is excluded from tax-supported institutions is coming from dogmatic educators who identify their own philosophy with ultimate truth. The natural outcome of an unwarranted exercise of freedom is to have it taken away. If academic freedom of testimony to one's own conviction should be restrained, American life and education would be immeasurably poorer. But we could not discharge the responsibility placed upon us in the preparation of this document if we did not declare our conviction that negative religious dogmatism in the schools is as un-American as positive religious dogmatism. Indeed, in the long run it may be more vigorously resented.

DIVERSITY OF EXISTING
POLICIES AND PRACTICES

U<small>P TO THIS</small> point we have not questioned, except by occasional inference, the assumption underlying most discussions of this subject that there is a definite American pattern of school relationships which prescribes the status of religion with reference to education. It is of no small moment, however, that existing practices in American communities are anything but uniform and do not, in themselves, define a broad policy. Any proposal put forward that involves giving some place to religion in the school program is regarded as a departure from a precedent which might be expressed by the slogan, "No religion in the schools." But an examination of the facts discloses no such condition. In fact, no aspect of the American situation is stranger than the disparity between what we say and what we do.

This in itself is not necessarily an indictment. If there were no reason for questioning the principle of secularization, it might well be maintained that departures from it in practice are but evidences of imperfection and that the goal is to keep them at a minimum. But, when an alleged precedent is appealed to as sanctioning the principle, the case is different. Let us consider some of the diverse practices.

Bible reading in the schools is an illuminating illustration. The number of states in which the reading of the Bible is required almost exactly equals the number in which it is prohibited! Together they account for about half the states in the union. Thus, in a nation recognizing a common set of political principles, diverse practices are authorized. Where Bible reading is required or permitted, it is regularized formally by the stipulation that there is to be no instruction connected with it. Thus, the principle is formally preserved while a concession is made to a demand that *some* religion shall be incorporated in the school program. As to the net spiritual result there is much skepticism among educators, but that question is not considered here. The conspicuous lack of consistency is what we are emphasizing.

Furthermore, in some states more explicit forms of worship are prescribed, and in innumerable instances simple services of worship are conducted with evident community approval. Again, school credit is allowed in many states for Bible study conducted outside the school. There are also school systems in which religious classes are conducted in the school, as part of the school program, by co-operation with church bodies, the cost being defrayed by private contributions. On the other hand, weekday religious education conducted under the auspices of churches and synagogues requiring only a minimum of school co-operation, a system which has achieved a high degree of public approval, encounters in some quarters serious opposition as an infraction of sound principle.

The most conspicuous example of religious observances in the schools is found, of course, in the annual festivals such as Christmas, Thanksgiving, and, latterly, the Jewish Hanukkah, in which the religious elements are undisguised.

The nearest approximation to uniformity is probably in the matter of restricting public education funds to public school use. But even here practice ranges from strict observance of this rule to furnishing textbooks out of public funds to pupils in parochial schools and providing free transportation for them.

It can hardly be doubted that these divergent practices which demonstrate the absence of an American policy with reference to religion and public education are themselves profoundly revealing as to the confused state of mind of the American people. Those who are irked by any raising of the issue seem to be trying to find a uniformity that does not exist. And it is lacking because there is wide awareness of a problem that has not been solved.

The situation, however, may be interpreted as indicating that there is in fact an "American way" in education with respect to religion, namely state and local control, with freedom to experiment. This is as it should be. Public education in this country is a function of the states, whose policy is to delegate control in large part to the local community. The advantages resulting from this decentralization are enormous. But with respect to religion the exercise of local initiative is hampered by fear of infringing some national policy or precedent concerning the relation between church and state. There is no such explicit precedent. We should like to see more trust imposed in the people to manage their schools, under prescribed academic standards, in their own way.

CHAPTER IX 〜

THE SEPARATION
OF CHURCH AND STATE

THE CONFUSION to which we have referred is further evidenced in the failure to give clear and definite meaning to the doctrine of separation of church and state outside the educational field. The confusion in education is part of a larger confusion. We have already testified to our concern that the control of public education be kept in public hands. That in itself evidences our conviction that the separation doctrine has a hard core of reality and is not to be disparaged. But it is essential that it be understood not as an absolute — which it tends to become in much current controversial literature — but as a broad principle of varying application, the essence of which is the preservation of maximum religious freedom. In particular, it is at the moment quite as important to note what, in actual practice, the separation of church and state does not mean as well as what it does mean.

The first point to observe is that even separation in terms of control is a relative conception. There is no such thing as a completely free church in a free state. The church is subject to the state in a variety of ways. It must obey building codes and fire laws. It must pay taxes on those portions of its property not used for purposes defined by statute as exempt. It must pay its debts. It even depends on the state for its legal incorporation, without which it would be powerless to hold and administer property. All along the line religious freedom, like other kinds of freedom, encounters limitations. Separation from the state is, therefore, a relative matter. This is not to lessen its importance; on the contrary, it is the more important to study its proper implications.

By the same token, the converse of this relationship — the activities of organized religion which affect the state — cannot be brought under a rule of thumb. Here, to be sure, there is greater divergence of opinion. Organized religion, composed, be it remembered, of people who are at the same time citizens having in common with other citizens a stake in the integrity of public policy, tends to be socially conservative. Some religious bodies have manifested a great reluctance to engage in activities directed toward influencing public policy on the ground that the church should avoid all semblance of political action. Even here, however, notable exceptions occur, as in the case of the prohibition movement, and also in respect to local campaigns for clean government. Churches and synagogues have taken an increasingly active interest in the political aspects of international relations. There is a trend, as previously noted, toward greater recognition of the propriety of nonpartisan political action on the part of religious bodies. This appears to be true of public opinion generally as well as of opinion within the churches.

A curious paradox which should be noted in passing is the applause accorded exceptionally liberal pronouncements by religious bodies on social and political issues by persons who continually warn of the danger of any departure from the principle of separation of church and state. It is evidence that even these persons have a broader conception of the matter than their slogans suggest. As in many other controversial matters there is probably wider fundamental agreement on this issue than appears in heated debate.

Be that as it may, religion in America today plays a considerable role in governmental affairs. This is true not only in respect to the kind of activity above referred to, but even more conspicuously in respect to specific religious services. The employment of chaplains in the armed forces at government expense is at present the most noteworthy example. The maintenance of religious services in public hospitals and prisons, the use of the Bible in administering oaths, the issuance of religious proclamations and calls to prayer by presidents or governors — these and other practices indicate how far short of a definite prescriptive rule of practice the separation of church and state is in America.

An important consideration is the very great variety of local conditions that affect policy. The crux of the matter is that while the commitment against sectarian teaching in the schools remains strong, what is actually sectarian is beyond legal definition and subject to *de facto* determination. Anything of a religious character that inflames one portion of the populace against another can readily be brought under the sectarian category. If no disturbance results, the probability is that a vigorously sponsored innovation will "get by." Democracy often works that way though it is undeniably hazardous. Many crimes against liberty have been committed with the shameful approval of the populace. That is why we value the Bill of Rights, maintained by a high central authority immune to local corruption.

We do not suggest that those who regard the introduction of religious subject matter into the schools as inherently destructive of freedom should abate their opposition in deference to a principle of local control. We do urge, first, the abandonment of an appeal to nonexistent precedent in support of an extreme secularist position; secondly, a frank facing of a problem that is all of a piece with the extension of democratic control of education and with the steady widening of the scope of the school program.

The core of meaning in the doctrine of separation of church and state we believe to be this: there shall be no ecclesiastical control of political functions; there shall be no political dictation in the ecclesiastical sphere except as public safety or public morals may require it. This doctrine may not be invoked to prevent public education from determining on its merits the question how the religious phases of the culture shall be recognized in the school program.

WEEKDAY RELIGIOUS EDUCATION

WE HAVE referred to the practice of releasing school pupils for attendance at classes in religious education held either in nearby churches and synagogues or in the public schools, as one of the ways in which communities have sought to compensate for the omission of the teaching of religion from the school program. It is important to understand the relation of this plan to the broad problem we are attempting to analyze. The recent rapid growth of the movement is one of the evidences of public concern for religious education. Furthermore, the fact that it involves a certain amount of co-operation on the part of the school administration indicates that in the communities where the plan is in operation there is recognition of an obligation on the part of public education to facilitate the conduct of religious education. This has an important bearing on the question discussed earlier of the responsibility of the community as a whole to promote an appreciation of the religious phases of the culture. No detailed discussion of the released-time movement is attempted here, but certain generalizations seem warranted.

First, weekday religious education is a community enterprise through which parents may take the initiative in getting more adequate religious education for their children in their own faith. It provides an opportunity for churches and synagogues to effect an extension of their own educational programs with public school co-operation. As such it makes no pretension to be non-sectarian, as we have used that term, but is an effort to strengthen the work of the church and the synagogue in their own fields. It is not to be confused with the function of the public school. Its indefinite extension would not of itself modify the conception we are here defending of the scope and adequacy of the public school program. At most it would be complementary. To the extent that the released-time plan increases the effectiveness of organized religion in the nurturing of its youth, this cannot fail to react on the school situation, but it would serve to emphasize further the educational dualism that secularization of the schools has brought about.

Secondly, we think no essential principle is violated by the released-time plan, as long as it is operated within the limits of the school laws of the state, and under the principle of local option in matters not specifically covered by the law.

Deserving of further comment, because of its controversial character, is the question whether or not such released-time classes should be held within the public school buildings. The following considerations are advanced: On the side of opposition are those who maintain that such a practice involves the use of public funds for sectarian purposes; that it is undemocratic because it separates pupils into sectarian groups within the school; and that it lays an unfair burden on school administrators to ask them to provide for giving children over to teachers not under their supervision while the pupils are still in their care. Those who favor the practice maintain that where use of public schoolrooms is necessary for the effective holding of released-time classes, granting such use is but a necessary part of the school's co-operation in a community plan for providing religious education; that separation into sectarian groups for religious instruction is but a recognition of sectarian divisions which already exist in the community and are known to every child; that this separation into sectarian groups may be used as a means of teaching positive appreciation of each other; that it is easier for school administrators to discharge their responsibilities when pupils remain in the school building than it is when they are released to churches and synagogues which are often many blocks distant from the school. On the merits of these two positions the committee makes no attempt to pass judgment, insisting only that whatever plan is adopted represent the will and purpose of the community concerned, expressed through appropriate channels.

Finally, the appraisal of weekday religious education in terms of actual results is primarily the responsibility of those conducting it, not of the public schools. The community, however, has an obligation to determine whether its merits are such as to justify its maintenance as a joint enterprise within the community involving co-operation of the public schools and the churches and synagogues. This will involve scrutiny of standards as to teaching personnel, curriculum, and equipment, as well as an appraisal of relationships between public and religious schools.

This whole matter of religious education on released time has attained such proportions that it calls for thorough study and evaluation. However, we repeat that the released-time program is not directly related to the problem with which this report is concerned. We are addressing ourselves to the responsibility of the schools in their own right, and in relation to their own program.

CHAPTER XI

THE BASIC RESPONSIBILITY OF THE PUBLIC SCHOOLS

WE HAVE sought up to this point to make clear the grounds of our conviction that the over-all situation with reference to religion and public education in America is not satisfactory and that the exclusion of religious matter which so largely prevails is neither required on grounds of public policy nor consistent with sound educational principles. Having put forward our view to this effect, we recognize an obligation to suggest possible developments in the school program that will be in line with the position we have developed.

The point of departure in the restudy of the curriculum from the viewpoint we have presented is the obligation of the schools to give the young an understanding of the culture and an appreciation of the ideals, values, and institutions which the culture cherishes. As has already been pointed out, appreciative study of the cultural heritage does not sanctify it. A better way to say this, perhaps, is that the capacity and the inclination to re-examine what is given in the inherited tradition are themselves among the most precious of our cultural possessions. Without them the social heritage would be unmanageable. But we hold no program of general education to be adequate that leaves any large area of human concern untouched.

What, then, is to be the goal of the study of religion in the schools, if there is to be such study? It is frequently said that teaching *about religion* is not teaching religion, and that the public school can make no contribution in this field because it is obliged to stop short of anything significant or worth while. In part this may be repeating an error that we pointed out earlier, namely, assuming that teaching in any field where there is sharp divergence of views means selecting one among alternative positions and "plugging" for it. Even so, to limit teaching to areas in which there is substantial agreement would leave education powerless at the cutting edge of a changing culture. The difficulty here would perhaps have been avoided if the term "study religion" had been used instead of the term "teach religion." Old habits of thought are hard to overcome even for educators.

But there is a sense in which the objection noted above is relevant and significant: the difference between acquiring information about a subject and having a meaningful learning experience is real and substantial. There is wide agreement, as we pointed out earlier, that significant learning is an active process. It culminates in "acceptance to act upon. . . ." It is for this reason that we often hear it said that character, or religion, or democracy cannot be *taught*, but must be *caught*. We think it much more in line with experience to say that the "catching" of such qualities of life as are implied in such a statement is itself of the very stuff of the learning process and is at the heart of the educational enterprise. Indeed, this is implicit in the emphasis on activity in modern educational theory. But to recognize this aspect of learning makes the distinction between *learning about* and a complete *learning experience* very real and important. The current interest in religious education will not, and should not, be satisfied with acquiring a familiarity with religious history or even a familiarity with religion as empirical fact in community life. The position we are taking requires us to face this inadequacy of mere objective study. To do so, however, only serves to make explicit our conception of all wholesome education as induction into the life of one's world through continuous meaningful and rewarding participation. Where this is not going on, something less than an adequate education is occurring. In its broadest sense religious education implies induction into the life of a religious community, commonly represented by the church and synagogue, which necessarily stand apart from the public schools.

How, then, can we expect much of the school in the sphere of religious education? Those who express skepticism at this point are raising no superficial issue. Yet we think the answer is not far to seek.

To begin with, even the most fundamental learning experience includes "learning about," and often begins in that way. One cannot enter into a friendship, or enroll in a school, or join a church without preliminary acquaintance. The first step in the acceptance of anything new is orientation toward it. Due to the secularization of life and education, contacts with religious life and activity tend to become less frequent and a vast ignorance of religion prevails. If society is really concerned, as we believe it increasingly is today, that religion should have a more important place in the lives of its youth, a first step is to break through the wall of ignorance about religion and to increase the number of contacts with it. Let it be freely acknowledged that this involves the basic assumption made earlier that religious activity is a normal aspect of life, just as truly as vocational work and political activity are normal aspects of it. Not any and all religious activity, to be sure; but neither can any and all vocational or political activity be given social approval and be encouraged in the school. The first obligation of the school with reference to religion is, we believe, to facilitate intelligent contact with it as it has developed in our culture and among our institutions. The many attempts that have been made in various states to overcome the effect of secularization bear testimony to a popular demand that the schools shall not ignore the claims of religion upon human life.

It is a grave mistake to suppose that the public school, holding as it does in so large part the power to determine the scope of intelligent interest and concern on the part of youth, can be neutral in this matter. The failure to play a part in acquainting the young with the role of religion in the culture while at the same time accepting such responsibility with reference to other phases of the culture, is to be unneutral — to weight the scales against any concern with religion.

We wish to stress as strongly as we can the belief that no education culminates worthily that does not result in convictions that will guide people in the use of their intelligence, their acquired knowledge, and the resources supplied by their environment. All education involves choices, both on the part of the educator and on the part of the student. Democratic education maximizes the role of student choices as free decisions. But freedom in a real world requires knowledge of the assets and liabilities of the culture in accordance with the broadest consensus of what the good life is. It also requires the capacity to think, judge, and act decisively. It is not the business of public education to secure adherence to any particular religious system or philosophic outlook. But we believe it is the business of public education to impel the young toward a vigorous, decisive personal reaction to the challenge of religion.

It is often complained that the younger generation today lacks convictions. We are in no position to make a quantitative judgment on this point. But to the extent that it is true, it is an indictment of education — not because young people have not been told what to believe but because they have not been irresistibly challenged to make up their minds, to achieve a faith, and to throw the weight of their lives into the struggle to vindicate it. Public education may not propagate religious dogmas or arbitrate religious differences. But if it does not impel students toward the achievement of a faith and to that end create a sensitive awareness of the religious resources upon which men have learned to rely, it is less than education ought to be.

ACTUAL POSSIBILITIES
WITHIN THE PUBLIC SCHOOLS

WE COME now to the crucial question: What can be done in the way of religious study within the public schools? An obvious answer, in the light of some of the facts already presented, would be that in certain communities almost anything seems to be possible. With respect to such situations we wish to say frankly that we hold no brief for every practice that now obtains. We have tried to make clear the dangers to religious liberty involved in sectarian indoctrination in the public schools even where community sentiment endorses it. We recognize that the principle of local control involves the hazard that unwise things will be done. Democracy always involves this hazard. But we are addressing ourselves to the problem that arises in the more typical American communities where the population is religiously heterogeneous and where sectarian differences are marked.

The first thing to be said is that in all probability there are communities where the situation is so rigid that no innovation could be attempted without a degree of friction that would nullify any gain to be experienced from it. Advances in public policy have to come about by experimentation where the community is ready for it. What we here suggest is based on the belief that where the will exists it will prove feasible to solve through co-operative effort the problem created by secularism. Only those, of course, who recognize the problem will be interested in any proposal whatever.

The logic of the situation points to the social studies as furnishing the most conspicuous opportunity within the schools below the college level. We are fully aware that some social studies text-books touch upon certain aspects of religious history and religious groups, but they deal with religion in an inadequate, if not in a very superficial, way. Serious attention to this deficiency needs to be given by textbook writers.

In the study of the various phases of community life — govern-ment, markets, industry, labor, welfare, and the like — there would seem to be no tenable reason for the omission of contem-porary religious institutions and practices. Here is an opportu-nity for a typical social studies project involving observation, in-terview, and research, and giving firsthand contact with the re-ligious life of the community on the basis of free inquiry. It will in no way commit the school to a particular sectarian position. There are school systems which have used this method, but illus-trations of it seem to be very few. It has the advantage of offering pupil initiative and affords an opportunity for independent study. It is not our purpose in this report to propose specific methods to be employed in a social studies program. However, we think that there are large possibilities in it which might be further explored.

Some religious groups do not welcome exposure of their chil-dren to the ideas, beliefs, and practices of other faiths. However, they must admit that the study of contemporary religious insti-tutions is a practical method for bringing the churches and syna-gogues in the community to the attention of millions of public school children who do not participate in the activities of the churches and synagogues. All seek an increase in friendly atti-tudes and a lessening of prejudice. There can be no progress in any of these respects except through closer acquaintanceship. We believe that this should begin as soon as students are capable of understanding the differences and will not be confused by them. It must be characterized by mutuality to the extent of a genuine desire to know one's neighbors better, to understand what they believe and why. This does not mean that a boy or girl of one faith is expected to modify his or her religious convictions. It means only that there is a will to understand. If we in America are seriously bent on reducing group prejudices, we cannot ignore the possibilities of creating good will through this kind of educational experience.

If members of any religious group in a community are not prepared to enter into such a program of mutual inquiry, we believe it will be amply rewarding to those who are. So far as we know, all religious groups welcome the study of their own faith by others. Let co-operation go as far as it will. Here, as in all matters where religious education is involved, the right of nonparticipation must be held inviolate.

The study of the religious classics, not in special religious classes but in the regular literature program, has not been entirely neglected, but provision for it is all too inadequate. The English classics are recognized as carriers of our cultural heritage. It can hardly be contested that the Bible is second to none among the books that have influenced the thought and ideals of the Western world. There is much evidence that the study of the Bible as a unique piece of religious literature, conducted with at least as much respect as is given to the great secular classics, and devoid of arbitrary interpretations to the same extent that we expect in connection with the latter, could be carried on without offense to any section of the community. We believe that teachers of English literature in large numbers would welcome the opportunity to make greater use of Biblical literature in their programs — and to prepare themselves accordingly.

We suggest that a careful study be made by teachers of English literature, assisted by Protestant, Catholic, and Jewish scholars, of the materials required to give students a reasonable degree of familiarity with our great religious classics. It is to be expected that the amount of time given to this portion of our literary heritage will vary widely among school systems. Guidance will be needed so that the best use may be made of available time. A commission constituted as above suggested would also be in a position to recommend suitable provision in the teacher-education program for this extension of the literature curriculum. We regard these suggestions as in line with some of the best current educational thought concerning the content of a liberal education.

If the Bible as such is to be studied in the school, the question arises at once: What account is to be taken of a religious objection to reading or listening to the text of a version of the Bible that is not approved by ecclesiastical authority? The problem is not merely one of individual conscientious objection, but of official objection. Full account should be taken of it. To say this, of course, implies disapproval of the legal requirement existing in many states that the Protestant Bible be read in school assemblies. It is a fair question whether such a legal requirement is not a violation of religious liberty. One way in which the situation has been met is to encourage each student to use the version which is approved by his communion. To some extent this is being done. Another way is to use secondary Biblical sources — Biblical narratives retold. From a literary point of view this is less desirable, but it is nevertheless a method by which familiarity with the content of a religious classic may be acquired.

When study of the Bible is mentioned as appropriate for the public school, the question is often asked, Why not the Koran, and the Chinese and Indian classics? The suggestion is in order provided we keep our sense of proportion. No educator with any knowledge of cultural anthropology would expect Egyptians or Turks to give as much attention to the Bible as to the Koran, or the Chinese as much as to Confucius, or the Hindus as much as to the Bhagavad-Gita. Our youth stand in the tradition of the

Western world, and there is every reason why they should know best their own classics. A better case can be made for the study of portions of the rich store of Talmudic literature which contributes much to an understanding of the Old Testament. To the extent that the study of other religious classics can be a vehicle of intercultural understanding and good will it might well find a place at appropriate age levels.

It should not be necessary to offer here a complete inventory of possibilities to be explored for giving attention to religion in proportion to its place in the culture. Mention may be made, however, of history, sociology, psychology, economics, philosophy, literature, music, and the fine arts. In part this list is relevant only to the higher education level, where, as we shall point out in a later section, the demonstrated possibilities of religious study in tax-supported institutions are much broader than at lower levels. In the study of music and the fine arts probably much more has been accomplished on the elementary and secondary levels than in any other field toward introducing religious subject matter, for the simple reason that it has been impossible to ignore it. This should be instructive all along the line. It suggests the irrelevance of much of the argument directed against religious subject matter as too controversial to touch. Religious art is full of dogmatic implications, but we have not heard it complained of as a cause of sectarian strife in the schools.

In history, in the sciences, and in philosophy, religion comes into the picture in ways that may indeed give rise to concern if we take counsel with our fears rather than our courage. Here the shoe will often be on the other foot; for much that has gone by the name "religion," as we have already pointed out, has been a reactionary force. But if we are serious about bringing religious subject matter into the schools, we must be ready to face the consequences of objective study of the religious phases of these various disciplines. It is a disservice to religion to oppose such study when it is competently guided by men and women who themselves have an appreciation of the role of religion in human life.

Certainly, on the higher educational level there would seem to be little reason for hesitancy on the part of religious leaders to assent to what is here suggested, in view of the greater maturity of the students and the widespread antireligious indoctrination to which we referred earlier. A deliberate and competent attempt to deal adequately with religion in history and science classrooms would tend to eliminate the one-sided and partisan teaching in a number of departments of which complaint is so justly made.

Let there be no misapprehension here. We want no abridgment of liberty. The competent scholar must be free to express his beliefs and his doubts in his field of specialization. But he has no right to give a spurious finality to his own views on religion by exploiting his academic prestige. In the long run fairness and adherence to sound educational practice do not curtail freedom, but enhance it.

In this discussion we have suggested nothing in the way of formal study of religion. In general, we think this is appropriate in public education chiefly on the higher level, and it will be discussed later. Indeed, the reference made to specific disciplines in the foregoing paragraphs does not imply that they should be taught as formal "subjects." In respect to curriculum theory we are not here concerned with controversies over the way subject matter is organized for study, but, so far as the present inquiry is concerned, we believe that a total orientation toward religion as part of the culture is better accomplished if religion is not abstracted from those fields of study, however designated in the curriculum, of which it is a part.

It is of the essence of our position that religion is inseparably bound up with the culture as a whole. Some religious groups, notably the Catholics, aim to achieve this synthesis in their parochial schools. They insist that the doctrines of religion be integrated with every subject in the school curriculum. To confine the teaching of religion to separate "religious courses" tends toward the very secularization we have argued against — the splitting-off of religion from the rest of life.

On the other hand, the essence of the secularist contention with reference to education, whether put forward by ardent churchmen or by persons who have no sympathy with religion, is that religion and public education belong apart. When, therefore, antisecularists advocate putting into the school curriculum separate courses in religion, which would in the nature of the case be elective, they may be perpetuating the secularist pattern by which religious subject matter is separate from everything else. The systematic study of religious history, of comparative religion, and even of religious doctrines may fit very well into the elective program of a state university, but even there it is no substitute for the study of the religious phases of the major academic disciplines.

CHAPTER XIII)✑

THE IMPORTANCE
OF TEACHER EDUCATION

THE IMPORTANCE of the teacher in the difficult task of relating religion and education cannot be overemphasized. Fortunately, there is already in the public schools a substantial nucleus of teaching and administrative personnel who are well informed in the field of religion and who live and teach on the basis of fundamental religious assumptions. They are to be found among all religious groups and could be trusted to teach religion without prejudice and sectarianism. The fact that the number of such informed teachers is tragically limited is a hazard which must be overcome if the task is to be accomplished. Two dangers loom large in the process: first, the danger inherent in the fact that there are large numbers of teachers who are not adequately informed in matters of religion and who lack interest in the study of religion; and second, the danger arising from the fact that teachers with deep religious convictions are tempted to teach religion along sectarian lines. These dangers are not insurmountable and do not represent vulnerabilities which cannot be overcome by good teacher education.

The answer to the question where the teachers are coming from is therefore obvious. They will have to come from the same sources from which we get teachers now, or from which we expect to get them in the coming years. This is not to exclude the possibility that in school systems which now provide for the conduct of religious classes within the school under church auspices, or in released-time educational plans, teachers may be found who can qualify as public school teachers quite as well as many who are now on the school payrolls. In many cases this is undoubtedly true. But probably most of the teachers thus employed would need further training in order to fit into the kind of program we have sketched, for it cannot be too strongly emphasized that this program is not something to be *added on* to the school curriculum, but rather something to be integrated with it. By and large, the task we have in mind, certainly below the college level, is one for which the teacher-education institutions of the country will have to prepare the larger part of the leadership if the task is to be done.

This does not mean, of course, that a wholly new corps of teachers must be trained for the work described. As already stated, there is good reason to believe that large numbers of our teachers would welcome the opportunity to broaden their equipment in order that the departments of study for which they are responsible may be correspondingly enriched. If the general point of view of this report is accepted, it will be evident that we are now failing to tap a substantial resource in educational leadership — a resource that goes unrecognized so long as we think of religious education as separate from every other kind.

New ventures in education have to be undertaken by co-ordinating teacher-education programs with local experiment and demonstration. Neither the teachers college nor the local school community can pioneer alone. It is probably safe to say that the readiness of school boards, administrators, and teachers to experiment is the best stimulus to new departures in the teachers colleges. On the other hand, demonstrations carried on by the latter have a potent effect in instigating community action. There is evidence today of an awakened interest on the part of school administrators in the problem we have been presenting.

In institutions where departments of religious education are maintained for the purpose of training professional workers in the religious field, there is already a base of operation. Here courses and workshops of a service type can be conducted by staff members who are regularly engaged with professional courses, with a view to giving members of the student body a background in religious ideas and religious history. This is not an innovation; it has been done with some measure of success. It requires little imagination to see the possibilities of further development through planned study for teachers of English and the social sciences who desire to work along the lines we have suggested.

In general, a department of religious education can probably function best by having on the staff members of different religious groups. It is hardly possible to do justice to all the elements of the Judaeo-Christian tradition, which must be understood in order to discover the religious roots of Western culture, by an exclusively Protestant, Catholic, or Jewish approach. Co-operative study is not only more productive of scholarship; it is a great solvent of prejudice.

It should not be necessary to say that all ideas of carrying through such developments as a crusade should be nipped in the bud. The task we have outlined is not one to be accomplished in any such fashion. Education cannot be forced. The equipment of teachers for the work they are now doing is a process that has undergone slow evolution. The profession on the whole tends to be conservative, though less so, probably, than the communities that many teachers serve. But the broadening of the school program has been, nevertheless, an impressive phenomenon. We believe there is a readiness, largely unsuspected, on the part of teachers to follow wise leadership on the part of the teacher-education institutions in the religious field.

CHAPTER XIV

RELIGION AND EDUCATION AT THE COLLEGE LEVEL

WHILE THE contemporary concern over the relation of religion and education focuses mainly on the public schools, the broader educational approach to the systematic study of religious subject matter forbids the exclusion of higher institutions from consideration. In the first place, any serious attempt to introduce religious content into the public school curriculum depends in large part, as has been indicated, upon a type of teacher education which has oriented prospective teachers to our great religious heritage. In the second place, in spite of clearly defined differences, there are striking similarities between the situation in our publicly controlled colleges and universities and that in public educational institutions in general. In the third place, the historical record of higher education is highly illuminating in relation to the problem as a whole.

The differences between public higher education and elementary and secondary education are very important, and it might be well to catalogue some of them at the beginning of this discussion. The maturity of college students is greater, and, it may be argued with some logic, the danger of religious indoctrination is less. These more mature students may be considered either to have formed their religious beliefs or to be at a stage where their critical judgment will enable them to insist upon more than a one-sided presentation of the subject. Moreover, the college community is more coherent and self-contained. Its activities are not objects of constant public concern, and the disconcerting pains of intellectual growth and development are not taken home daily to parents. In brief, to a considerable extent the colleges and universities absorb their own shocks. These and other factors tend to make the problem of developing the implicit relation of religion to education in the colleges much simpler than in institutions below the college level.

There is a long tradition in this country of religious orientation at the level of higher education. The early colleges were founded and supported by the churches. They served as the agents of culture and of religion on a wide frontier. Because of the difficulties of transportation, denominational rivalry, and the American principle of universal education, there was a conscious decentralization of educational facilities and, therefore, a multiplication of colleges. In many respects the colleges and churches co-operated to meet what they called the "spiritual necessities" of a new country. They did more than that; they played an important part in the formation and perpetuation of the secular elements as well as the religious elements of the culture. Thus, religion and education joined hands, and together they traversed and conquered a continent.

These frontier church-related colleges, modeled after those of the East, set the pattern for education at the higher level for many decades. Even those institutions which have subsequently severed all legal connection with religious bodies frequently preserve a hospitable attitude toward things of the spirit. While the seed of publicly controlled higher education was sown during the colonial period, it was the Revolutionary and post-Revolutionary periods, as contrasted with the colonial era, that saw the rise of the state-university movement. However, these new institutions had yet to make their case with the American people. The movement lost ground around the turn of the century due to a resurgence of religious influences, but was positively assured of its place following the passage of the Morrill Act of 1862. Nevertheless, in the process of growing up, public higher education was destined to be influenced by religion beyond the expectations of its most sanguine prophets.

This historical perspective will help to explain why the factors that brought about the secularization of public education at the elementary and secondary level were less significant at the higher level. Moreover, churches and synagogues have continued to exercise a large measure of responsibility for organizing and maintaining religious interest on the campus. College religious associations have had a recognized place on practically all campuses. Whatever the state regulations regarding the teaching of religion may have been, there has been little disposition to question the propriety of religious interests and activities. They have had official encouragement in many instances and at least official tolerance in the rest.

Let us not hastily assume, however, that the relations between education and religion at the college level are satisfactory. To be sure, custom and differences previously noted make it somewhat easier at the higher level to expose students to the religious elements in the cultural tradition and to the religious values which many hold as basic to a tenable philosophy of life. Nevertheless, the tide of secularization which has been pronounced throughout the whole of life in this century has engulfed some of the erstwhile academic strongholds of religion. The disintegration of the religious outlook has been due in part to the increasing emphasis on the intellect and the things of the intellect as the primary concern of the college. The increase of knowledge in the nineteenth century, the establishment of the free elective system, the influence of the German universities, the demand of an increasingly complex society for technical experts — all conspired to focus attention upon the importance of imparting knowledge and upon "training." In so far as these factors represented the growing-up of American institutions of higher learning, they are to be viewed with satisfaction. But it must be noted that the shift in interest and emphasis supported, without design, the secularist trend.

Many of the extreme secularists of this generation are to be found on college and university faculties; for within that large and influential group, much of the scientific work and most of the reflective thinking about science are done. While we have maintained that there is no necessary conflict between religion and science, we have also argued that what we believe to be a misinterpretation of the role and significance of science has given a major impulse to the development of a secularist philosophy. The significant point here is that the issue over the scope and adequacy of science and its relation to religious faith has had its major battleground on the campus. This is important, for the impact of the secular disciplines on religious thought at the higher and graduate level reverberates throughout the whole educational system.

No thoughtful person would question for a moment either the serious purpose or the significant results of science. It has made such magnificent progress in expanding our knowledge of the universe and in giving us control over the forces of nature that its prestige is unchallenged. Too many of its devotees, however, have been blinded by its very glory into making quite unwarranted claims for it. We are told, for example, that the scientific method is the only avenue through which values may be apprehended. We are sometimes informed that only the objects with which science deals are real, and that all else is superstition inherited from a pre-scientific age. This is a wholly untenable position. The moral values or ends by which men guide their lives cannot be verified by the scientific method, with its appeal to facts as the corroboration of previously framed hypotheses or its reliance upon the statistical and mathematical approach to the description of phenomena. Religion involves a concern for ultimate truth and a devotion to ultimate ends that man has no facilities for validating, in a factual or strictly empirical sense, either in the laboratory or elsewhere. This qualitative difference between religion and science is recognized by eminent scientists, as well as by philosophers.

Even the scientific enthusiast, who tries to bring all human experience under his laboratory categories, acts in many of the most significant areas of his life with a minimum of guidance from his scientific store of knowledge and a maximum of dependence on his moral impulses. The distinction to be noted is not between scientists and men of faith, but between scientists as such and scientists as men. Obviously, both the scientific urge and the moral springs of action are essential. Action without past experience is blind, but action without moral imperatives is below the human level.

Nevertheless, there have been many who were all too ready to claim for science a monopoly on human wisdom. The disease of "scientism" has been widespread in academic circles. The scientific method, developed in the field of natural science, has been applied to social studies where, to be sure, it is applicable, though limited with respect to quantitative measurement. But it has also been introduced into the humanities, where its application is by no means clear and where it has confused the issues. It has made curious beings of many college teachers who, because of their profession of scientific objectivity, dare not express a conviction. It has been said that in the realm of values they were neutral between right and wrong. They have tended to regard religion as purely a private matter, consisting chiefly of a set of individual beliefs — or aberrations. This tendency to look upon religion merely as an individual concern we have already seen to be one of the evils of a secular age. The higher learning in America has developed a broad urbanity, an all-engulfing tolerance, which finds it easy to be hospitable to everything except conviction — and genuine conviction, which must not be confused with intolerance, is one of the crying needs of our age.

It should be noted that a wide variety of conditions exists in tax-supported higher institutions. It is, therefore, especially important not to apply a common stereotype to all campuses in this matter. In actual practice two general patterns appear, one putting the responsibility for religious initiative and action on religious bodies and agencies whose activities are extra-curricular, and the other centering it in the administration and the faculty. An ideal arrangement would preserve the voluntary, extra-curricular aspect, while promoting the official responsibility. At the present time it is all too common for the administration to point to the various religious groups and agencies with the belief that provision for religion is adequately made. There is no substitute for official concern, and no agency will be so effective as a body of men and women on the faculty who care about the ultimate ends of life and who, in class and out, are prepared to stand up and be counted.

Broadly speaking, we believe in the same principle of divided responsibility for the college and university which we advocate on the lower age levels. The educational institution should take responsibility for the adequate study of religious institutions, history of religion, and in particular the relation of religion to world-order, not merely in isolated courses but as aspects of a human institution. It should also provide opportunities for worship services. The cultivation of particular religious traditions and their conscious promotion are the task of the church or synagogue, working in close association with voluntary campus organizations. In addition to formal instruction, the teacher has an opportunity to make his influence felt in the classroom, in the dormitories, and on the playing fields. Colleges and universities should encourage members of their faculties to participate in this kind of informal education.

Religion at its best has two major aspects: on the one hand it thrusts outward, tending to universality; on the other hand, it individuates, developing intensively in particular forms. Its perennial problems are to prevent the universalistic strain from being merely a weak diffusion, and to prevent the individuating tendency from becoming exclusive. Because religion brings into close association both those concerned with the ultimate ends of life and those devoted to science, the institutions of higher education have a special mission to fulfill. Because they have responsibility for the young men and women who seek to become educated human beings, they have a special task to perform respecting the total culture. While there are encouraging features in many colleges and universities, it remains true that an indigenous and authentic concern on the part of the institution to overcome religious illiteracy, to rediscover the religious roots of culture, and to help students to develop a religious philosophy of life by which they may live, indeed, has not yet developed.

CHAPTER XV

THE SCHOOL, THE CHURCH, AND THE HOME

BECAUSE IT is often contended that the effort to introduce the study of religion in the schools is at bottom an attempt to create an alibi for the church, the distinction between the functions of the two institutions in this connection needs emphasis. It is no part of our intention to make the one carry the burden of the other. On the contrary, we see in the suggested program a means of enriching both. If attention to religion as an aspect of the common life were not, as we see it, fully warranted on educational grounds, quite apart from its effect on our religious institutions, this report would never have been written. On the other hand, if we did not believe that organized religion stands to gain by the developments we propose, we should have less confidence in the effectiveness of our appeal.

To begin with, the church and synagogue, like all other institutions, are dependent on the school for the basic educational equipment of the people they serve. The claims of business, industry, labor, and the professions upon the schools are freely recognized. To be sure, they have to be kept in balance. But to the extent that the schools have failed to lay an adequate foundation for vocational work, they have heard from those elements of the community most concerned. The present controversy over vocational education is a striking illustration. The new interest in work experience is a result of the impact of the world of work upon the world of education. This is as it should be. No group, no institution, may demand special favors of the schools, but every kind of organized interest and activity that has broad community sanction may properly expect that the schools shall not be unmindful of the phase of human interest and concern which it represents. Community demands on the schools, which from time to time bring about adaptation of the curriculum, rest on this principle.

What stake, then, have the church and synagogue, as such, in the school program? Simply this: that youth should be made appreciatively aware of those aspects of individual and social living which, with abundant social sanction, they have sought to serve. The effort to remove impediments in contemporary culture to social and spiritual progress has had wide approval from many of those who are most vocal in their opposition to any religious elements in public education. The social justice crusades of the churches and synagogues arise out of the fact that their ethical message is stifled by organized forces in society that obstruct the growth of the human spirit. These are the historical fruits of secularism, which denies the relevance of religion to life. Precisely the same concern motivates religious leaders who, with a firm fidelity to the public schools, nevertheless find in the secularization of education a force that steadily drives religion into the background of human concern. Those who object to other-worldliness in religion should recognize that this dualism is enshrined in a secularist culture.

The idea that the churches are asking the schools to do their work is due to a misreading of the facts. Many churchmen joined ranks with the secularists long ago in supporting the exclusion of religion from the schools. This report is addressed as much to church people as to any other group. If the churches and synagogues of America were fully convinced of the implications of the secularization of education, the popular mood would reflect that conviction in a stronger demand for its correction. We see our task in preparing this document as one of making articulate a concern which is growing in America, but which the churches are far from grasping in its full significance. When they do become aware of it, they sometimes seek ill-devised remedies. It would be difficult to find more vigorous denunciation of all efforts to introduce the study of religion into the schools than has come from some liberal churchmen. This fact, we think, with all respect, only illustrates the way in which the secularist outlook has invaded the church itself, with resulting confusion. These liberal churchmen are among the foremost champions of social justice and of the social expression of the religious impulse. They are characterized by a fine and generous insight into the spiritual worth of men and women who stand quite outside the religious community — and who sometimes put to shame those who are in the church but not of it! This very urbanity and breadth of outlook tend to minimize in their thinking the importance of institutional religion. We believe the religious structures of society, that is, the institutions of religion, are at least as essential to the permanent maintenance of religious faith and mood of mankind as other institutions are to the perpetuation of the interests they serve.

This conviction, of course, is not shared by those to whom secularism is not only a policy but also a way of life. To them the school itself may seem to be in some sense the temple of the community's highest aspirations. If they are right, religious institutions, as such, will probably tend to atrophy and disappear. We contend that such an assumption is foreign to the mind and mood of the American people as a whole and that educational policy cannot be built upon it.

In any case it should be clear that in contemporary society the church and synagogue perform functions in the conduct of corporate worship, the nurture of growing persons in a particular spiritual fellowship, and the maintenance of a discipline of life in accord with a particular set of convictions, which can in no way be confused with the function of the school and could not be taken over by it. The schools aid the church today by giving to youth an appreciation of fundamental spiritual values to which we have referred. They might aid it much more by giving to youth an orientation toward the specifically religious phases of human culture. And they might remove a definite disservice to the church which results from the devaluation of religion that is implicit in ignoring it.

The primacy of the home as ideally the most effective of all educational agencies is no more impaired by what we propose than is the status of the church. It is true that part of what we are asking the schools to do — to lay a foundation for intelligent religious interest — can be accomplished in the home, and often is. But just as the school in a hundred other ways is daily called on to compensate for the deficiencies of home life, so in respect to religion it may be a responsibility of the schools to compensate a cultural defect in many American homes. In the weekday religious education program this principle is already recognized, since the initiative comes from the parents. Unless we misconceive the whole problem, the function of the home in religious education will on the whole be amplified, not reduced, by the performance of what we believe to be the function of the school.

It should go without saying that if and when anything suggested in this report is construed by parents as violating liberty of conscience their wishes should be deferred to. We realize that this is not so simple a matter as in the case of particular classes which one may attend or not. The incorporation of religious subject matter in the regular study program affects the whole body of students. Hence the proposal must stand or fall in accord with the reaction of the general public. It would seem, therefore, that any contemplated plan should be thoroughly discussed and evaluated by citizens, boards of education, representative community groups, and perhaps by special advisory commissions. If the community as a whole is not persuaded of its essential validity, it cannot be done.

CHAPTER XVI

THE SPIRITUAL REPLENISHMENT OF MODERN CULTURE

We BEGAN this report with a characterization of modern culture as secular in the sense that it segregates religion from the common life. We now return to this theme in order to appraise our cultural deficit. The argument thus far has been based on the logic of the total educational situation rather than on definite claims concerning what changes the study of religion might be expected to make in the national character. Critics of all such proposals are fond of pointing to the fact that nations which have turned out to be notorious mischief-makers have been at great pains to instruct their children in religion. We hold that no *a priori* judgment of the result of such a program of religious education as we are advocating is possible. The integration of religion with the total process of general education has not been accomplished in modern times. The schools might conceivably succeed in their part of the task and the churches and synagogues fail in theirs, precisely as a superb piece of political education in the schools might be frustrated by the activities of political parties. We who write this report are members of religious bodies to which we owe allegiance by conviction. For us, the democratic faith means that the worth of persons and the increasing perfectibility of human institutions rests on a religious conception of human destiny. We believe that the Judaeo-Christian affirmation that man is a child of God expresses an authentic insight which underlies all particular theological formulas. We further believe that many of those who are fighting valiantly for the democratic cause under wholly nonreligious slogans are unconsciously trading on "borrowed capital" that has been furnished by the religious tradition of the culture. We think the effort to sustain a social ethic that has been severed from its cultural roots will not succeed generation after generation. That rootage is not merely in concepts and articles of faith but in the ongoing corporate religious life of our people. Yet believing all this, we repudiate all intolerance of persons who support democracy on wholly secular grounds.

What we do contend insistently is that in the effort to build a democratic society a failure to capitalize the ideas of ethical monotheism, the teachings of Judaism and of Christianity, the tough fibre of that integrity which made the church resist, more effectively than any other institution, the Nazi tyranny in Europe —a failure to preserve such great assets is sheer cultural madness. It is, to be sure, largely the fault of the churches that religion in the Western world appears not as a unifying, but as a divisive, force. But underneath the cleavage between Catholic and Protestant, between Christian and Jew, is the stream of the Judaeo-Christian tradition with its conception of the common source and spiritual equality of all men as the children of God; the obligation to respect the supreme worth of persons and the wickedness of exploiting them; the golden quality of mercy; the meaning of redemptive love; the inexorableness of the law that he that soweth the wind shall reap the whirlwind. These are great cohesive spiritual forces to which the secular order of society probably owes more than it suspects. The practical question that confronts statesmen and educators in a time of great cultural upheaval is what steps shall be taken to use the obvious resources of our religious tradition and the institutions that foster it. This is no time for an irrational alliance between complacent churchmen, actuated by fear that the state will impair their ecclesiastical independence through the instrumentality of the common schools, and extreme secularists, who see in institutional religion only the preservation of superstition. We face a condition, not a theory.

On all sides we see the disintegration of loyalties, the accentuation of partisan strife, the revival of ancient prejudices, the increase of frustrations, the eclipse of hope. It is not our purpose to assign any single cause for these cultural and personal ills, or to propose any single solution. The issue is not whether any of us know the right answers; on that we shall never agree. The issue is whether we shall take stock of our cultural possessions, find the springs from which our people draw their spiritual sustenance, and, from them, irrigate the waste places in our common life.

Educators are increasingly stressing the need for guidance and counseling directed toward the integration of personality on higher levels of responsible living. Discerning treatises are written about the causes of frustration and the disintegration of personality. Religion at its best has always been an integrating force, a spiritual tonic for a soul wracked by fear and cringing in weakness. It is one of the marks of a secular age that scholarly and earnest persons who seek to fortify the human spirit are unmindful of the greatest resource that mankind has known. To those who are convinced that religion has little to offer and that true progress can come only by secular means, we say only that every man must find the altar of his own soul and that the people have erected their altars throughout the land. Religion in America is an empirical fact. As such, it is marked by many imperfections, but it embodies the faith of the majority of the people. Its imperfections will not be lessened by an attitude of splendid isolation on the part of intellectuals, or of indifference on the part of those responsible for the education of youth.

It is worth noting that all reforms that come to fruition in history are motivated out of the past. There is always a harking-back to the ideals of a former age, to the tradition of the fathers, or to a lost sense of destiny. The imperative toward moral betterment comes out of a common heritage. Even if in the iconoclastic zeal of the moment everything belonging to the historic past is derided, there comes a time when ancient tradition is appealed to for guidance in the new day. True, time makes ancient good uncouth, but without the ancient good we should be chartless on a stormy sea.

SUMMARY AND CONCLUSIONS

WE HAVE endeavored to state the problem arising out of the secularization of American life and education. Before it can be solved, careful studies will need to be made of local community situations, of various types of experimentation now going on, of professional and lay opinion, of the legal questions involved, and of the experience of other countries. It is our intention to initiate studies of this sort to the fullest extent possible. In this report we have attempted the preliminary task of stating the problem in a context of educational principles.

In brief, the problem is how to find a way to give due recognition in public education to the place of religion in the culture and in the convictions of our people while at the same time safeguarding the separation of church and state. A solution, as we see it, requires the charting of a middle course between the existing situation and the adoption of expedients which are unwarranted. The exclusion of religion from the public schools which so largely prevails today results in its relegation in the minds of youth to a position of relative unimportance. This runs counter, we believe, to the intention of the American school system from the beginning. On the other hand, any educational innovation which would tend to identify public education with a particular body of sectarian beliefs and practices we hold to be not only impracticable but improper.

We have drawn a distinction between secularism as a philosophy of life, which owes nothing to historical religion in any form, and the divorce of religion from everyday human affairs. We do not believe that the American people or American educators are committed to an irreligious, secular philosophy. Rather, what has come about in the modern world and in the educational system is the isolation of religion from the daily concerns of business, industry, and politics and from the educational disciplines designed for our youth. Holding to the principle of the separation of church and state in America, we nevertheless deplore what we consider a strained application of that principle in our school system. We are unable to believe that a school which accepts responsibility for bringing its students into full possession of their cultural heritage can be considered to have performed its task if it leaves them without a knowledge of the role of religion in our history, its relation to other phases of the culture, and the ways in which the religious life of the American community is expressed. An educated person cannot be religiously illiterate.

It would be quite unjustified, of course, to contend that the secularization of modern life is wholly due to the prevailing educational pattern. Indeed, we have endeavored to show that for several centuries a process of cultural fragmentation has been going on, with the result that modern society lacks a unifying spiritual principle. It is our belief, however, that this process was very greatly stimulated by the artificial limitation of the school curriculum to nonreligious subject matter. That this process was occasioned by sectarian controversy for which religious bodies must largely bear the blame, we freely recognize. But this fact serves only to emphasize the possibility of a solution of a sectarian problem which will not be nihilistic with reference to the study of religion as a basic human concern.

It is far from our purpose to suggest that remedying what is here characterized as a fault of our educational system would in itself restore spiritual unity and integrity to the culture. There is no panacea for the spiritual ills of our age. We are convinced, however, that it is idle to attempt to recover for religion its essential role in social and personal living so long as it is denied recognition in the schools.

Growing dissatisfaction with the situation we have described has led naturally to a variety of proposals for its correction. To these we have given earnest thought, but while we have definite convictions about certain of them, we are convinced that the practical solution of the problem to which they are addressed awaits more extensive investigation and study. Concerning two proposals frequently advanced we have felt called upon to express a judgment.

Many persons believe it possible to distill from our major religious faiths certain common ideas and propositions to which the American people would overwhelmingly give assent, and make of these a common core of religious instruction. No doubt this could be done in many American communities. Indeed, it is being done in some school systems today. But we believe it objectionable from a religious point of view as well as on educational grounds. It seems to us that to pursue such a policy would be, at best, to assume that the support of an overwhelming majority of the people justified overriding the convictions of a minority. The rights of minorities must be protected if religious liberty as defined in American law and custom is to have any meaning. Not only so, but "religious instruction" of this sort runs counter to the trend of public educational practice in America, which disapproves indoctrination with reference to matters of belief.

Concerning weekday religious education, we have noted that it is peripheral to the subject of this report. We have been content to state the pros and cons concerning its most controversial phase — the conducting of sectarian classes in school buildings by representatives of the several faiths. It appears that new legal precedents may be established with respect to this practice which has been adopted in some communities. Many people believe that on the principle of local control of educational policy there is much to be said for such a program, as against a rigid secularization which excludes religion altogether. In this report, however, we have addressed ourselves primarily to possibilities which we think inherent in the present situation without statutory or constitutional changes, provided the statutes and constitutional provisions are subject to reasonable interpretation. We do not regard it as reasonable to construe a ban on sectarian instruction as prohibiting all study of religious subject matter.

Fundamental to the proposals we have set forth is an interpretation of "teaching" which distinguishes it from indoctrination in the ordinary sense of that word. We have recognized that religious indoctrination is widely practiced in our churches and synagogues. It is their right to practice it if they are so disposed. But in order to introduce the study of religion into the public schools, the teaching process must be understood in a different sense, the sense in which it is commonly used today in application to all study of controversial subjects about which reasonable people differ. We have frequently used the phrase "the study of religion" instead of "teaching religion" because the latter so commonly implies indoctrination.

In line with this understanding of what the teaching process involves in the religious field, we have suggested as one possibility including in the literature program, at the appropriate level, study of our basic religious classic, the Bible, in order that our youth may become familiar with the major literary sources of their religious heritage. It is scarcely possible to understand the central values of Western culture without a knowledge of the Bible. Study of it in the school, with whatever adjustments in the matter of texts used may be thought desirable, should go far to overcome the religious illiteracy of our time. Experience indicates that where the aim is to educate, not to proselytize, inhibitions dwindle away. Here, too, however, conscientious objection should be respected. To those who contend that the study of the Bible as literature is not religious study at all the obvious answer is that the Bible is *religious* literature and can be studied only as such. To use it as a basis for doctrinal instruction is the function of church, synagogue, or home, not of the public school.

We have suggested also that attention be given in the social studies program to the religious life of the community. It surely is as important that our children become thoroughly familiar with the activities and programs of the churches as that they learn the operation of banks, factories, and markets. Here again what we are suggesting is no substitute for religious education in the full sense of the term. Rather, it is aimed at a sympathetic acquaintanceship with religion as an aspect of contemporary life.

These are illustrations of an approach to a major educational problem. They are aimed at breaking down the barrier between the religious and the secular in the educational system. If such procedures are successfully undertaken they will lead naturally to the exploration of the religious phases of the various disciplines through which our children and youth pass at successive levels. We wish to see school boards, administrators, and teachers freed from fear of sectarian indoctrination in order that religion may be given attention wherever it comes naturally within the scope of the educative process.

One of our major concerns has been with the present status of religion at the college and university level. Here we find a paradoxical situation. On the campuses of some tax-supported institutions there is a great deal of religious activity and in many cases there are successful departments of religion. On the other hand, in the teaching of science and philosophy a mind-set often prevails against historical religion in all its forms. In many publicly controlled institutions of higher learning there prevails a superciliousness with respect to religion and an actual indoctrination against widely held religious convictions. This is an insidious intrusion of doctrine, a violation of the principle of religious liberty, and an abuse of academic freedom.

But if the free and untrammeled study of religious subject matter in the ways here suggested is to be made possible in the schools, teachers must be prepared for the task. This does not, in general, mean special teachers, but men and women who have not neglected the religious phases of the culture or of their several disciplines. The teacher-education institutions and the liberal arts colleges, which now furnish the majority of teachers in elementary and secondary schools, should assume responsibility for leadership in bringing this about.

The religious community itself, which must bear a large part of the blame for the extremes to which secularization has gone, has an important part to play in their correction. Everything we have suggested can be blocked or nullified by sectarian bitterness, suspicion, and fear. If our religious leaders have a serious concern over religious illiteracy and the secularization of life, they must give the educators freedom to enrich the curriculum of the schools in ways that are sound and wholesome. The schools belong to the people and they are bound to reflect the people's fears and prejudices as well as their aspirations. Broadly speaking, there should be a meeting of minds among religious leaders in the community before a school administration can be expected to move in the direction we have indicated.

This report is addressed to people who believe in the American school system, in which the authors also profoundly believe. We have sought to make it clear that we are in full sympathy with those who stress the spiritual values which are inherent in public education. Indeed, we consider the democratic aims of education which stress the immeasurable worth of persons, the values of mutual understanding, and the possibility of human fellowship across all racial and creedal lines as the flowering of the Judaeo-Christian tradition. To this extent our schools are undoubtedly engaged in a spiritual enterprise. It is our conviction, however, supported, we believe, by the vast majority of the American people, that in the long run the resources of religion are essential for the preservation of these spiritual values.

Religion is either central in human life or it is inconsequential. If it is not basic in experience and in the culture, then the secularists are right in their neglect of it, and the testimony of the ages is false. We believe otherwise; and we think the fruits of the secularization of life are becoming evident to the masses of our people whose changing mood is made articulate in the utterances of some of the profoundest thinkers of our time. The intensive cultivation of religion is, and always has been, the function of religious institutions. To create an awareness of its importance is a responsibility of public education. In creating such an awareness the school is but rounding out its educational task, which culminates in the building of durable convictions about the meaning of life and personal commitments based upon them. The school cannot dictate these convictions and commitments, but it can, and should, foster a sense of the obligation to achieve them as a supreme moral imperative and to that end bring its students into contact with the spiritual resources of the community. Let us abate none of our enthusiasm for scientific knowledge and useful skills, but let us remember that only a strong faith that can resolve the perplexities of life and a lasting commitment to high purposes will make education complete.